FESTIVALS TOGETHER

And joy is everywhere; it is in the earth's green covering of grass; in the blue serenity of the sky; in the reckless exuberance of spring; in the severe abstinence of grey winter; in the living flesh that animates our bodily frame; in the perfect poise of the human figure, noble and upright; in living; in the exercise of all our powers; in the acquisition of knowledge; in fighting evils... Joy is there everywhere...

Rabindranath Tagore.

Festivals Together

A guide to multi-cultural celebration

Sue Fitzjohn

Minda Weston

Judy Large

Illustrations by John Gibbs
with
Sarah Fitzjohn and Abigail Large

Original music by Jehanne Mehta

HAWTHORN PRESS

Published by Hawthorn Press,
1 Lansdown Lane, Stroud, Gloucestershire,
United Kingdom. GL5 1BJ

Typeset in Plantin by Glevum Graphics,
2 Honyatt Road, Gloucester. GL1 3EB
Printed by Butler and Tanner Ltd., Frome, Somerset.

A catalogue recording this book is available from the
British Library.

ISBN 1 869 890 47 7

PREFACE

This book is a gathering of celebrations, activities, songs and stories which reflect the diversity and life of our own particular community.

It can in no way claim to be a definitive work on multi-cultural festivals. It is one offering, and it is offered in the spirit of sharing and in the hope that readers elsewhere will be prompted to see what cultural richness is around them in their own areas.

Through festivals, music and stories, we discover what is universal and what is unique. We also discover each other.

Judy Large.

This book was made possible by the support, encouragement and creativity of many people.

Warm thanks to all the team:

Cherry Bevan, Leslie Collins, Sally Cocksedge, Ann Felce, Peter Fitzjohn, Fran Garcia, Jamila Gavin, Jane Grell, Barbara Imrie, Haruko Kinase-Leggett, Dr Kunijwak Kwawang, Richard Land, Jenny Lauruol, Ann Lewis, Gori Nanabawa, Charlie Ryrie, Patrick Roe, Kavita Sharma, Zippy Shiyoya, Veronica Walters, Jane Welch and Paul Wong.

ACKNOWLEDGEMENTS

Special thanks for support and assistance to:

Eve Barwell for text from *How to Make and Fly Kites* by Barwell and Bailey, Studio Vista, London 1972.

A & C Black (Publishers) Ltd. for traditional songs from the Caribbean as from *Mango Spice*, with Manley Young and Chris Cameron for words and music to "Anancy the Spiderman."

Rosamund Grant and Virago Press for material from *Caribbean and African Cookery*, London 1989.

The Islamic Foundation, Leicester, England for stories from *Marvelous Stories from the Life of Muhammed*, written by Mardiijah Aldrich Tarantino, Leicester and Nairobi, 1982.

Aban Bana for support and encouragement (Udwada Gam, Gujerat, India).

Joseph Jacobs and Dover Publications Inc. for "The Broken Pot" from *Indian Fairy Tales*, London, 1969.

Susan Smith for "Mother Holle's Cookie House" from *Echoes of a Dream*, Waldorf School Association of Ontario, Canada.

Further contributors include:

"How Ganesh got his Elephant Head" and "Lakshmi and the Clever Washerwoman" are reprinted by permission of Pavillion Books from *Seasons of Splendour* by Madhur Jaffrey.

The song "Prayer to the Prophet Muhammad" is from *Festivals*, copyright Jean Gilbert 1986. Reproduced by permission of Oxford University Press. Please apply for reprints.

Songs "Wahawi; ya Wahawi," "Ramadan is Come" and "Iroquois Lullaby" from Cass Beggs, *A Musical Calender of Festivals* by permission of Ward Lock Educational.

Extract from "Autumn Poems" by Fan Ch'eng-ta is taken from *Anthology of Chinese Literature*, ed. C. Birch and D. Keene, Penguin, 1967.

The harvest benediction from *Atharva Veda XII* is taken from *The Hindu Tradition*, ed. A. Embree, Random House, 1966.

Frontpiece quotation from Rabindranath Tagore is from *A Year of Grace*, ed. by Victor Gollancz, Penguin, 1955.

Instructions on musical instruments are adapted from the "Sounds and Movement" section of *Discovering with Young Children*, Ash Winn and Hutchinson, Elek Books Ltd., 1971.

Grateful acknowledgements also
to the following sources:

Sara Cone Bryant and George G. Harrap and Co. Ltd. for "The Whale and the Elephant" from *Stories to Tell Children*, (1918).

Jean Chapman and Hodder and Stoughton (Australia) for extracts from "In Candle Light" in *Pancakes and Painted Eggs*, 1981.

E. B. White and Harper and Row for extract from *Charlotte's Web*, 1952.

The Dominica Institute of Roseau, Dominica for songs from *Chance Domnitjen*, "Susie in the Moonlight."

The Great Britain China Centre London, and Chen Wei for extracts from "Chinese New Year Brings a Host of Festival Delights."

The Chinese Community Centre, London, Chinatown and Guanghwa Co. Ltd. for reference to "Introduction to Popular Traditions and Customs of Chinese New Year," published in 1986.

Jamie Stuart and the Saint Andrew Press of Edinburgh for extracts from *The Glasgow Gospel* (1992).

Carol Kendall and Yao-Wen Li for "The Thief who Kept his Hands Clean" from *Sweet and Sour: Tales from China Retold* Bodley Head 1978.

Tayeb Salih for extracts from "A Handful of Dates" from *The Wedding of Zein*, Heinemann Ed. Books Ltd., London 1979.

Bantam Doubleday Dell Publishing Group Inc. for "A Rootabaga Story" by Carl Sandburg from *The Family Treasury of Children's Stories Book Two*, Doubleday and Co., Inc. 1956.

Jamila Gavin and David Higham Associates for stories from *Stories from the Hindu World*, Macdonald, 1986.

Pinhas Sadeh and Collins for "The Wise Men of Chelm" from *Jewish Folk Tales*, 1990.

Ruth Sawyer for extract from *The Long Christmas*, The Bodley Head Ltd., 1964.

Camara Laye and Collins, Fontana Books for extract from *The African Child*, 1970 edition.

Kunijwok Kwanwang for "The Rabbit and the Crocodile," retold here by Jamila Gavin.

Paul Wong for traditional stories and Chinese harvest song.

Robin Crofts Lawrence for "The Prince of Butterflies" by Dorothy Harrar from *Nature Ways*, New York Rudolf Steiner School.

Every effort has been made to trace owners of copyright material, but in some cases this has not proved possible. The publishers would be glad to hear from any further copyright owners of material reproduced in *Festivals Together*.

CONTENTS

INTRODUCTION

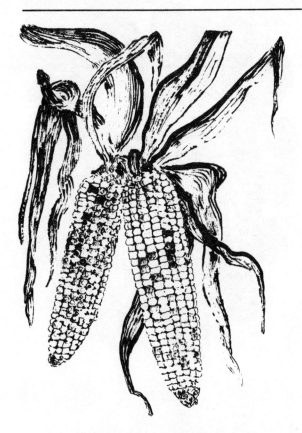

A note about weights and measures

The recipes in this book give quantities in US cups and metric weights and measures. Do not try and combine the two in a single recipe as the quantities do not translate directly. Where pints are also given these are British Standard pints, not American. If readers in the UK still prefer to use imperial measures, convert grams to ounces assuming 25g = 1ounce (i.e. 100g represents 4ozs; 150g represents 6ozs etc).

Richard Land, Headteacher, Widden Primary School & Family Centre, Gloucester, England.

A personal perspective

I would hope that my attitude and philosophy towards celebrating festivals would reflect the following quote from Jose Levine.

"We have to define an education which is hospitable to diversity. Education is about letting people be different, valuing them for their individuality and the unique characteristics of both individuals and groups — education is about enabling us to appreciate such varieties and differences. On the other hand, education is also about making people the same, education is based on some belief in the value of certain attitudes over others."

And similarly reflect the following quote from Martin Luther King Jnr.

"We have inherited a large house, a great 'world house' in which we have to live together — black and white, Easterner and Westerner, Gentile and Jew, Catholic and Protestant, Muslim and Hindu — a family unduly separated in ideas, culture and interest, who, because we can never again live apart, must learn somehow to live with each other in peace."

Schools are microcosms which reflect the macrocosm. In my years of teaching in St Paul's, Bristol, Duxford, Cambridgeshire and now inner city, Gloucester, I have used festivals as one important part of an overall strategy to affect positively the school as a microcosm in order, even if only in an extremely small way, to affect the macrocosm for change, and change in attitude for the common good. We talk about festivals in our whole school assemblies. We think of ourselves, the whole school, as a family. Attitude change comes from within. However, I am convinced that over time this can be achieved and achieved through sound education as part of the process of that change.

Different calendar dates

For simplicity's sake this book is divided into seasons as experienced in the northern hemisphere, but the festivals interweave here across the equator and across 'civil' calendar dates. Hence in the autumn harvest section there is a memory of harvest in Guinea quoted from Camara Laye's *African Child*. Camara Laye's text also reads:

"In our December, the whole world is in flower and the air is sweet: everything is young and fresh; the spring seems linked with the summer, and the countryside that for so long has been drenched in rain and shrouded in baleful mists now lies radiant; the sky has never seemed so blue, so brilliant; the birds are ecstatically singing… It was the best time of the year, the summer and all that it stands for, all it holds and cannot hold…"

This picture of December contrasts sharply with the North American or European experience of a particular month. But the ensuing description of men at work in skillful reaping strikes a universal tone which seems to defy civil calendars: that time of year when the fruits of labour may be gathered in and stored. So the seasons in this book are simply a framework into which can be gathered universal celebrations, so that we may translate them into our lives.

Calendar dates pose their own problems. For example Christmas in Australia will call up varying experiences and lore today. If memories of wintry northern customs still influence the 25th December in Australia, or New Zealand, etc., we must look forward to a new expression of this festival out of a different seasonal context. A richness of cultural interpretations may be found thus from South America, Sub-Saharan Africa, the South Pacific region and so forth.

The usage of the 'Roman' calendar dates back to Julius Caesar's abolition of the use of the lunar year and 'intercalary' (or intervening, compensating time) month. He fixed the mean length of the year at 365¼ days and decreed that every fourth year should have 366 days with others standardized at 365. Imperial decree standardized the names and lengths of each month as we know them today. But the religious world reflected cosmic understandings not so easily or rationally 'fixed'. For the western heritage this is reflected in Easter's movement each year according to the Christian world-view. This Ecclesiastical calendar was in fact both lunar and solar. The Council of Nicaea ordained in 325 that Easter celebration should take place on the Sunday immediately following the full moon on or nearest to the vernal equinox!

The festivals in this book reflect a diversity of ancient traditions and calendars which precede the Roman one. Here are a few introductions to these.

From China we have the world's oldest lunar calendar. Traditionally there are about 29½ days from one new moon to the next with 12 revolutions of the moon making 354 days. An intercalary month 'Rùnyuè' was inserted every two and a half years. The solar calendar was important in official matters and the four seasons were vital in philosophical, religious, and social custom. Modern People's Republic of China does use the western calendar and officially places New Year on 1st January. But Chinese communities world-wide will vary the celebration time according to tradition.

There are twelve months in the Hindu year, each having 30 days making a year of 360 days. To correct for the missing 5+ days another intercalary unit, 'Adhik' is added every few years. But festival dates do move according to the moon.

Hindu month — Corresponding Western month:

Chiatra	— April
Vaishakh	— May
Jayshyth	— June
Ashadh	— July
Shravan	— August
Bhadrap'd	— September
Asvin	— October
Kartik	— November
Margashersh	— December
Paush	— January
Magh	— February
Phalguna	— March

Islam traces its calendar to that given to Muhammed on his last journey to Mecca. The twelve lunar months use about 11 days less than a solar year, and approximately every 33 years the months pass through a circle of a whole solar year. Months are seasonal and dependent on the sighting of the new moon. Each year festivals will keep to the lunar pattern, moving forward 11 days, ie:

First day of Ramadan / Eid-ul-fitr / Eid-ul-Adha:

4 March 1992 / 3 April 1992 / 10 June 1992
22 February '93 / 24 March '93 / 31 May '93
11 February '94 / 13 March '94 / 20 May '94
31 January '95 / 2 March '95 / 9 May '95
20 January '96 / 20 February '96 / 28 April '96
9 January '97 / 8 February '97 / 17 April '97

And so forth…

Names of the months in the Muslim calendar:

1 — Muharram
2 — Safar
3 — Rabi ul-Awwal
4 — Rabi ul-Akhir *or* Rabi ul-Thani
5 — Jamada al-Awwal
6 — Jamada al-Akhir *or* Jamada al-Thani
7 — Rajab
8 — Sha'ban
9 — Ramadan
10 — Shawwal
11 — Dhu l-Qi'da
12 — Dhu l-Hijja

The Jewish calendar is lunar, 12 months beginning at the new moon and lasting 29 or 30 days. There is an intercalary month 'The Second Adar" but the ancient ritual calendar has a solar basis. Year dates are historically specific, and 1995 will be Jewish year 5756.

Jewish month— Western calendar:

Tishri	— September/October
Cheshvan	— October/November
Kislev	— November/December
Tevet	— December/January
Shevat	— January/February
Adar	— February/March
Nisan	— March/April
Iyyar	— April/May
Sivan	— May/June
Tammuz	— June/July
Av	— July/August
Elul	— August/September

So much for technical background to moving festivals. The real purpose of this book is to deal more with their essence, and related activities to share. It will not be difficult to find relevant specific dates for your own time and place. So, in the words of the Rabbi sending congregation members out for the Succot ulav and etrog, "Go and find the best you can."

And enjoy it!

References:
Camara Laye, *The African Child*,
Collins, London 1970, p.46.
Celia Collinson and Campbell Miller,
Celebrations: Festivals in a Multi-Faith Community,
Edward Arnold Ltd., London 1985.

An Ibibio tale

As a rule, young children will have less difficulty grasping lunar dates than adults. To them it is obvious that the sun and the moon are constants in a daily cycle, and that the moon alone regularly waxes, wanes and beams full again in a rhythm of its own. In very built-up urban areas the sun and moon still link the child with the world of nature.

But how did sun and moon find their sky places originally? One possible explanation of events long ago comes to us from eastern Nigeria, an Ibibio tale.

Long, long ago, the sun and his lovely wife the moon lived down on the earth. The sun was great friends with water, and often visited the house where water lived. They would spend many hours talking together. But the water never visited the sun's house, and one day the sun asked his friend:

"Why do you never come and visit my house? It does not seem right that I am always visiting you but you never come and call on us. The moon and I would be really pleased to welcome you and your family into our compound."

The water laughed. "Thank you, my good friend. Please don't be offended that I stay away. But I am afraid your house is not large enough. If I came with all my family, I'm afraid we would frighten you away!"

"We are planning to build a new compound soon," replied the sun. "If it is big enough, please will you come and visit us then?"

"I'm afraid it would have to be very large indeed for us to come, for my people and I take up a great deal of room," explained the water. "I fear that we might damage your home."

The sun seemed rather upset that water would never come and visit him, so water promised that he would try to come when the new compound was built. He did not want to upset his friend, but he warned that it would have to be a very big compound indeed, for his family was really very large.

So the sun and his wife the moon gathered their other friends together, and they built a magnificent new compound, with high wooden fences surrounding a large patch of land and many huts. Then the sun returned to his friend's house.

"Dear water," he said, "Please come and visit us now. All our friends have helped us to build a splendid new compound, and we would like to welcome you there."

The sun was so full of enthusiasm about this new compound, and wanted water to visit so much, that water felt quite unable to refuse his kind invitation. He was still worried, but arranged to visit the very next afternoon.

The next afternoon the sun and the moon prepared the compound for their friend. They tidied and swept, and made sure that everything was spick and span. At the agreed time the visit began. Through the gate into the compound water flowed. He didn't come alone, but brought with him hundreds of fish, eels and frogs, waterfowl and watersnakes, even water-rats and water-voles. When the water reached half way up the fence, he asked the sun: "Do you still want my people and me to come and visit you inside your compound?"

The foolish sun, not wanting to seem unfriendly, said "Yes. Oh yes, let them all come!"

So the water carried on flowing into the compound until eventually the sun and the moon had to climb right onto the top of the roof of their hut to keep dry.

"Do you still want us to come in?" the water asked again.

The sun didn't want to go back on his word to a good friend. Although he could see that the water had been right, there was no room, he still replied; "Yes, my good friend, I have invited you all to come in. Come in, come in!"

The water kept on coming, and before long it even reached the top of the sun's roof. To keep dry, the sun and the moon had to go right up into the sky. And that is where they have lived ever since that day.

*These craft areas are useful and enjoyable
throughout the year and may be adapted to
particular celebrations or themes.*

Claywork — *for lanterns and lamps.*

Papier mâché models — *for dolls or display.*

Musical instruments — *for rhythm and dance.*

Paper kites — *for festive flying.*

I
CELEBRATION CRAFT

1. CLAYWORK

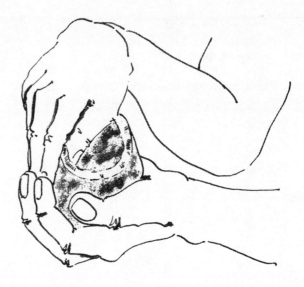

Making a clay lantern

Pinch or thumb pots are an easy and immediate way to start working in clay. It is most satisfying if you work slowly and rhythmically, all the work is done within your two hands, don't hurry as the warmth in your hands will help to stiffen the clay so that it will hold the shape you give it. It is fun to shut your eyes once you have started as it really is all done by feel at first.

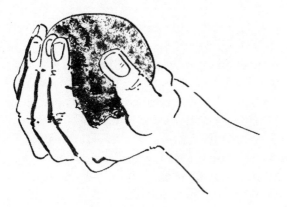

1. Take a small lump of soft clay. Shape it into a ball.
2. Hold the ball of clay in one hand, push your other thumb gently into the middle.
3. Squeeze the pot from the bottom gently between your fingers and thumb.
4. Don't let the top open out too much.
5. Continue pinching and stroking, turning the clay in your hand as you work.
6. Leave a thick roll of clay round the top of the pot until you are ready to make your final shape.

While children are slowly and rhythmically working the little pots, I tell this story about the first firing of clay pots.

Once upon a time, a long time ago in a far away place some children collected clay from near a river. They made little pots just like the ones you are making. The children finished the pots and put them near a fire at the entrance to the cave where they lived. They knew if it rained in the night their pots would just be muddy clay in the morning. In the night the pots rolled over into the embers of the fire. Very early in the morning it started raining. When the children woke up they went to see if their pots were turned to mud... what a surprise, they found the pots were hard and would even hold the rain water. The fire had changed the clay into pottery and I am sure this was a children's discovery.

When the pots are an even shape leave them to firm up a little. The children can now pierce holes in flower designs all around the pot. Use a pencil or sharp stick to make the holes. Make good clean holes big enough to let some light shine out.

When the pot is dry a small night light will fit inside and give a lovely pattern of light all around the pot.

These little lanterns do not have to be fired but if you have a kiln they will be much stronger fired.

The most important part of this work is that you all enjoy the experience of the clay and that everyone's efforts are valued. Have fun.

Sally Cocksedge.

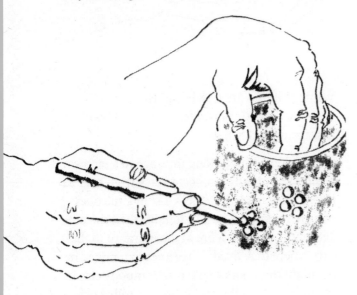

If you have kiln facilities, try modelling clay diva lamps for Divali in traditional shapes to hold standard night light candles, or dish-like candle holders for other festive times.

Mind how you treat your pot — lest it break, you'll lose the lot!

The story of the broken pot

There lived in a certain place a Brahman, whose name was Svabhavakripana, which means "a born miser." He had collected a quantity of rice by begging, and after having dined off it, he filled a pot with what was left over. He hung the pot on a peg on the wall, placed his couch beneath, and looking intently at it all the night, he thought, "Ah, that pot is indeed brimful of rice. Now, if there should be a famine, I should certainly make a hundred rupees by it. With this I shall buy a couple of goats. They will have young ones every six months, and thus I shall have a whole herd of goats. Then, with the goats, I shall buy cows. As soon as they have calved, I shall sell the calves. Then, with the calves, I shall buy buffaloes; with the buffaloes, mares. When the mares have foaled, I shall have plenty of horses; and when I sell them, plenty of gold. With that gold I shall get a house with four wings. And then a Brahman will come to my house, and will give me his beautiful daughter, with a large dowry. She will have a son, and I shall call him Somasarman. When he is old

enough to be danced on his father's knee, I shall
sit with a book at the back of the stable, and
while I am reading, the boy will see me, jump
from his mother's lap and run towards me to be
danced on my knee. He will come too near the
horse's hoof, and, full of anger, I shall call to my
wife, 'Take the baby; take him!' But she,
distracted by some domestic work, does not
hear me. Then I get up, and give her such a kick
with my foot." While he thought this, he gave a
kick with his foot, and broke the pot. All the
rice fell over him, and made him quite white.
Therefore, I say, "He who makes foolish plans
for the future will be white all over, like the
father of Somasarman."

2. PAPIER MÂCHÉ

Cloth sculpture

To celebrate special occasions, whether historical events or festivals, making these figures is a fun and inexpensive way of recording the event permanently.

Materials:

Cardboard (eg. old cereal boxes.)
Cloth (A variety of textures and colours, cotton being the easiest to handle. Thick wool and nylon are not suitable.)
Wire (Garden wire is ideal.)
Pliers
Cold water paste (Scola Cell by Play Art is good as it is non toxic and will not stain.)
Sellotape
Newspaper
Paint (Powder, poster, acrylic or gouache.)
Trimmings (Braid, buttons, fur, beads, wool for hair, lace.)

Getting started:

Decide on the overall finished height of the model that you are aiming for.

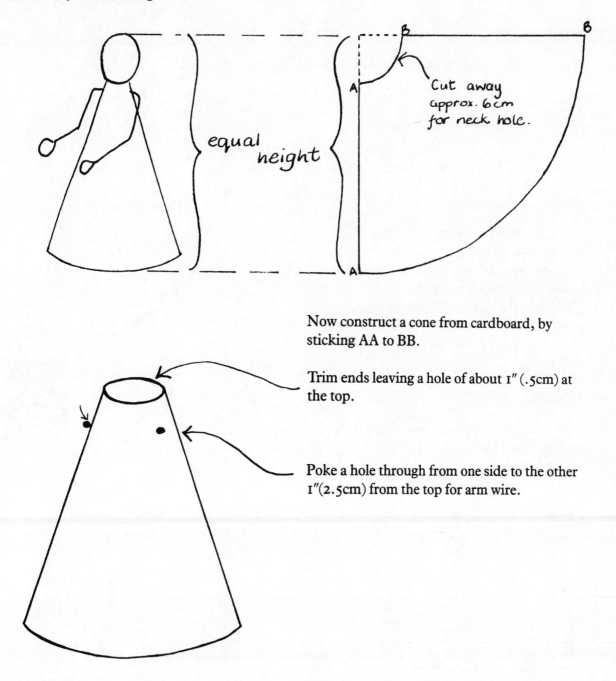

equal height

Cut away approx. 6cm for neck hole.

Now construct a cone from cardboard, by sticking AA to BB.

Trim ends leaving a hole of about 1" (.5cm) at the top.

Poke a hole through from one side to the other 1"(2.5cm) from the top for arm wire.

Cut a piece of wire three times the height of the finished cone.

Fold it in half and form a circle, using the top third.

Twist.

Poke the two ends through the holes, formed in the cone.

Bend the wire into required arm positions. Form hands and twist into position.

To make head and hands:

Make up paste in a bucket according to instructions on packet.
Crumple a ball of newspaper and push into circle of head wire and hands.
Using strips of newspaper dipped into the paste, cover paper ball, neck and hands.
Mould face, neck, shoulders and hands, leave to dry.

Clothing the figure:

Take a rectangle of cloth (choose colour and texture to suit character).
Cut as follows:

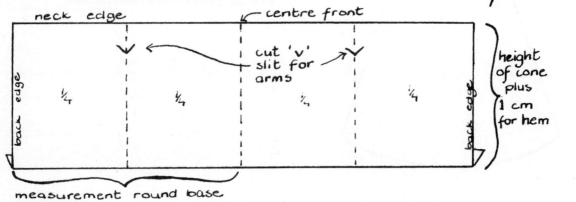

neck edge   centre front

cut 'v' slit for arms

¼   ¼   ¼   ¼

back edge   back edge

height of cone plus 1 cm for hem

measurement round base of cone

Applying the paste. (Treat all cut pieces in the same way.)
Dip the fabric into the cold water paste.
Squeeze the paste through the fibres thoroughly.

Remove surplus paste.
Open and smooth out cloth.
Put arms through slits in cloth.
Turn up raw edge on hem.
Arrange cloth into folds.
Smooth firmly around neck and close back seam.
For sleeves, cut a square of cloth either in the same colour or one chosen to contrast.
Paste triangles as before.
Arrange on model.

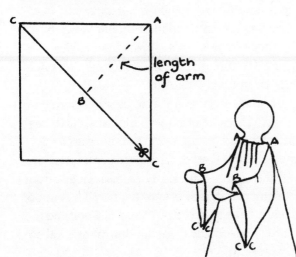

Giving your model character:

Collars, shawls, head dresses, hats and turbans can all be applied in the same way.
Cut squares, rectangles and circles of cloth and practise draping them on the model before pasting them.
Mix up some fairly thick paint, and paint hands, face and features.

And finally, trimmings:

Character and individuality can be achieved by imaginative use of trimmings.

For a nativity scene, figures can be made to appear kneeling by cutting a shorter cone, and careful arrangement of the cloth to suggest knees and feet. Hands can be carefully positioned to hold gifts or crooks.

Animals can be made by similar methods.

Cherry Bevan.

3. MUSICAL INSTRUMENTS

Drums and dances

The resounding tone of the drum gives a sense of occasion at ceremonies in festivals and other forms of celebrations. Rastafari friend Micheal Lennox describes the importance of the drum in the Caribbean and as a main sound and focal point in Rastafari gatherings. For the African heritage, drumming has been central to religious worship and ceremony.

Drummer Ben Baddoo suggests that music in Africa grows out of life and speech and that the relationship between language and music is so close that musicians make their instruments according to the language they 'speak'. This

means that musicians tune their instruments to the sounds that will regenerate the sounds of their mother tongue. Ben further explains that the precision with which language can be duplicated on musical instruments varies but the phenomenon exists throughout Africa, where drummers reiterate the sounds and pitch of African tonal language.

From the northern part of the Philippines, in the province of Abra, the 'Tinggians' or 'Itnegs' (my own native ancestors) use the 'gansa' or gong and the tambor (drum) to accompany our native dance — 'tadek'. The gansa is made from a strong metal, cast iron or copper. The tambor is made from a carved out block of wood and the drum head is made from the skin of the carabao or water buffalo.

The gansa and drums are beaten with either a stick or with bare hands, when one instrument compliments the rhythm of the other. The musicians are in full control and command the rhythm of the dance. 'Tadek' is a romantic dance, which conveys a long-winded courtship, and the story is not planned, but rather performed impromptu. It would normally start with the 'bidang' (scarf tied around the skirt) being thrown around, and whoever is nearest to where it lands is the one who has to get up and dance! I'm afraid, excuses are not accepted! The steps, actions and expressions in rhythm with the gansa and tambor are all made up, much to the delight of the audience. The dance would eventually end up with the bidang folded and exchanged. Unless the suitor is not accepted, in which case there is a mere shake of the hand.

The tadek is popular at weddings and just before the rainy season in Abra.

Drums

Improvise drums from yoghurt cartons, tins (use coffee and cocoa tins which do not have to be cut open and are therefore free from sharp edges), cardboard cylinders, round wooden date boxes or biscuit tins. A large coffee tin can have rubber stretched over the open end — the rubber from an old inner tube may be used. Or the membrane can be made from heavy duty polythene such as that sold for painting and decorating. A less durable drum can be quickly made using stout wrapping paper to stretch over the container. Experiment with other materials.

1. Draw a circle on the back of the material you have chosen. Make it an inch or two larger in diameter than the tin or carton.

2. Cut out the circle, lay it flat and place the open end of the container on it centrally. Draw round the container.
3. Spread glue on the underside of the material from the rim of the circle to the outer edge.
4. Stretch the material over the open end of the container pleating the overlap neatly, so that it is as taut as possible.
5. Bind the overlapped material with tape or string to hold it in place. This can be a temporary measure to hold the Fablon or rubber in place while it is sticking, or a permanent decorative feature. If the latter, ribbon or coloured PVC tapes can be used, or coloured string contrasting or

harmonising with the colour that the container is painted.

The drum can be struck with the finger tips to sound it, or simple drumsticks can be made:

Use a piece of half or quarter inch dowelling or bamboo for the stick. The length is a matter of experiment but it will not need to be more than eighteen inches. Make a tight ball of rags in a circle of chamois leather or a piece of old leather glove — push stick in and tie tightly; you could also push the end of the dowel into a cork or small rubber ball — possibly securing with glue.

Based on material in *Discovering With Young Children*, Ash, Winn, Hutchinson. Elek Books, London 1971.

Stringed instruments

A simple stringed instrument may be made using a wooden base with regularly spaced saw cuts in the narrow ends. Stretch nylon washing line tightly between these. Knot a piece at one end and thread it through the saw hole so that the knot prevents it from slipping through, pull it tightly over the board and knot the end on the other side of the opposite saw cut. The bridge should be a thin strong piece of wood and if it is inserted at an angle the varying lengths of string obtained will produce different sounds.

Elastic bands stretched between nails on a board will also produce a sound when plucked; or stretch them over stout cardboard or plastic boxes.

Clappers

Wooden cigar-boxes give out a pleasing clonk when struck. The plastic tops of sprays, or any such hollow form, when struck on wood give a satisfying clopping sound. If a coconut is available, the shells can be cut in half and struck together or with a stick, or covered with Fablon to make a drum.

Rattles

Rattles can be made from plastic bottles. Put in a quantity of rice, beans, peas, nails, small stones or gravel, or macaroni to make different sounds. The bottle can be corked, or a handle made from dowelling or any piece of cylindrical wood of a diameter to allow it to fit firmly into the neck of the bottle, where it can be secured by glue. All these rattles can be decorated with paint and finished off with a coat of varnish.

Jinglers

Some traditional peoples make rattles and jingling bracelets from sea shells and nut shells. On the beach, collect shells, looking particularly for the ones with a hole worn in them. Thread them on to separate lengths of nylon thread or thin pieces of string, four or five inches long, with a knot tied in the end so that they do not slip off. Fasten the thread to a loop of tape which children can hold and space them so that they jingle together when shaken. You can do the same thing with nut shells. If walnuts are cracked carefully half the shell can be used. Pierce the hole for the string with a bradawl. Or use small metal washers, beads, or bolts.

Bells

Bells are excellent for rhythm with dancing. They can be bought at most toy shops and sewn to tape, fastened to wire or stapled to the end of a stick. They are effective around ankles for marching or jumping to time.

Ask around for people in the community who would bring and demonstrate traditional instruments! This can be inspiring and enlivening!

4. PAPER KITES

Kites

Here in the West, windy days are associated with autumn, when brown and golden leaves are flying in the wind. While in the East, kite flying can be part of a festival as in India in February, in Japan or in China. In the Philippines the 'ullaw' (kite) is the most important toy of a child during October and November when windy days coincide with rice harvesting. Imagine a field of yellow rice, swaying and dancing with the wind while on the bank by the field a child flies a kite made of manilla paper, creamy in colour. The colour of the kite blends with the colour of the ripening rice but soars upward to stand out against the blue of the sky.

Kite flying is also enjoyed in the open city parks of Manila where brightly coloured kites are flown on Sundays in October and November.

For very young children, a basic simple kite may easily be made in the classroom from stiff card and coloured tissue paper.

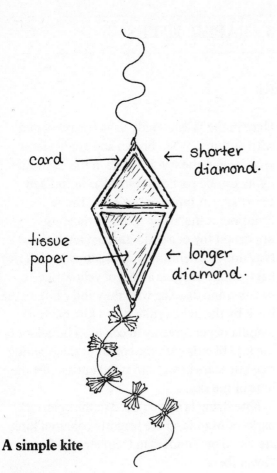

card → ← shorter diamond.

tissue paper → ← longer diamond.

A simple kite

Stiff cards
Brightly coloured tissue paper
Glue
String

1. Cut out diamond shapes from the stiff cards.

2. Cut out 2 triangle shapes from the diamond.

3. Then cover both triangles with brightly coloured tissue.

4. Make a tiny hole at the top of the smaller triangle, and then thread the string through.

5. Decorate the kite with a tail if preferred.

Cardboard kites are especially suitable in the classroom where there are no bamboo sticks available.

Six steps in kitemaking

How to bind and glue the sticks:

Wherever two or more sticks cross they must be tied and glued together. This gives the kite a really firm framework.

Lay the sticks in position. Tie on a piece of string or cord.

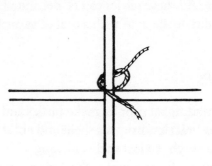

Wind the cord round the join like this...

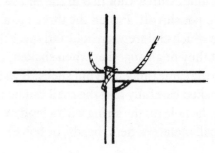

...then like this.

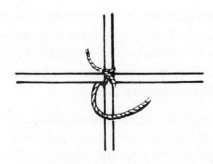

And then weave it round, over and under the sticks like this.

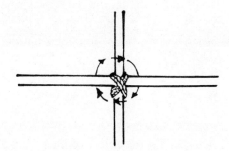

Cover the cord with dabs of glue. Leave it to dry.

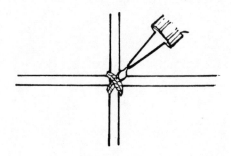

How to frame the kite:

Most kites need a frame of string or cord. It helps the kite keep its shape and makes a firm edge for the cover.

Cut a notch in the end of each stick like this.

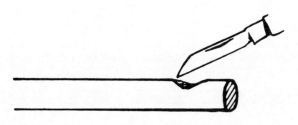

Tie a piece of string to one of the sticks. Leave a fairly long end.

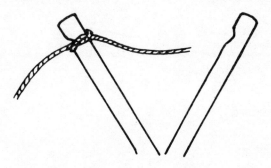

Keeping the string taut, take it across to the notch on the next stick and wind it round two or three times.

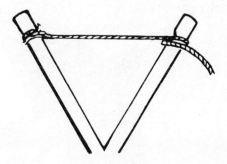

Wind the string round all the sticks in turn until you are back where you started. Tie the two ends of the string together.

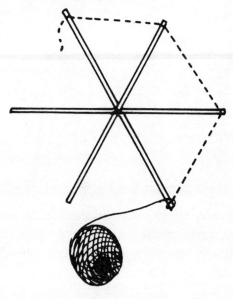

(For a cutter kite, cut the notches like this. Simply slot the string into the notches and pull it tight before you knot the two ends together.)

Bluebird

You need:

2 sticks the same length
1 bendy stick rather longer than the other two
A short firm piece of stick
Paper and glue
String and curtain ring
Paints, crayons or felt pens

1. Lay out the two identical sticks and the short firm piece in the shape of an 'A'. Bind and glue the sticks together where they touch.

2. Lay the last stick across the 'A' and bind and glue it in position.
3. Attach a string to point 'b' and tie the other end to point 'c' so that the cross stick is bent. Tie another string from 'd' to 'e'. Make sure that each wing is bent the same amount.
4. Cover the frame with paper.

Bridles:

Cut one piece of string to reach from 'c' to 'x' and back to 'e'. Tie the ends to points 'c' and 'e', looping the string through the curtain ring as you do so. Cut a second piece of string to reach from 'c' to 'x' and tie it to the tops of the wings at the points marked 'y', again remembering to loop it through the ring.

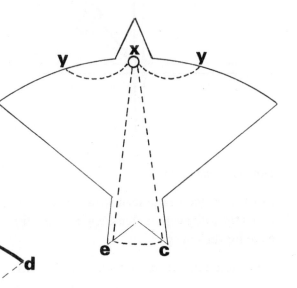

Tail:

Make a tail about three times the length of the kite. Tie a loop of string from 'c' to 'e' and hang the tail from it.

Decoration:

Paint or draw the feathers onto your Bluebird.

The centipede and butterfly

Two little sisters went walking one day,
Partly for exercise, partly for play
They took with them kites which they wanted to fly,
One a big centipede, one a great butterfly
Then up in a moment the kites floated high,
Like dragons that seemed to be touching the sky!

Chinese traditional.

II
SPRING

II

SPRING

1. CHINESE LANTERN FESTIVAL

Chinese Lantern Festival

Teng Chieh, the Lantern Festival has traditionally marked the formal end to New Year celebrations and the beginning of Spring. The return of longer days, more light and warmth along with the onset of the growing season are marked at this time. Lanterns are hung from high poles and carried in procession. They take on imaginative form in shape, size, colour… Some representing animals, birds, and very importantly, the dragon. The high point of traditional celebration is the parade or dance of the dragon. The creature is made on a long framework of bamboo (up to or over 100 feet long!) and covered with bright paper or silk.

Ancient texts record lantern festivals of up to five days long, as in the Song Dynasty (tenth to thirteenth centuries). Temples, homes and trees were strung with lanterns for dazzling light and beauty as soon as dusk came. Coloured glass or even white jade were used for these, and sometimes they were painted with landscapes, human figures, flowers or birds. Here is a poem written over five hundred years ago by Xin Qiji on such a festival occasion:

An easterly breeze prompts a thousand
*   trees to bloom at night,*
It also blows them off, which fall
*   like a rain of stars.*
Carved cabs drawn by steeds leave
*   the whole street a pleasant smell.*
The flute is heard in the air,
The light of the jade-like lanterns
*   are glittering.*
All night the lanterns of fish
*   and dragon keep dancing…*

Folk Customs at Traditional Chinese Festivities, Beijing, 1988.

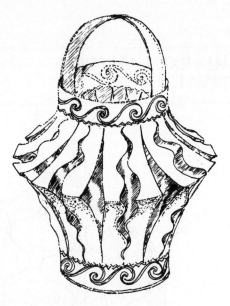

How to make a Chinese Lantern

You will need:

A rectangular piece of paper (which can be coloured and decorated as you wish).
A narrow strip of paper.
Some glue and some scissors.

1. Fold the rectangular piece of paper in half lengthwise:

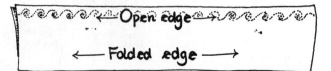

2. Make cuts (straight and/or wavy) along the folded edge, ending 2cm from the open edge:

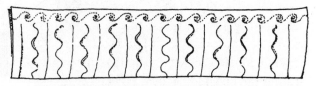

3. Open out the paper.
4. Bend the paper to make a cylinder and glue the two short edges together.
5. Attach the narrow strip of paper as a handle.

In traditional times the Lantern Festival occasioned the reopening of government offices and courts of law after the New Year Festival. Here is a story of a law court of long ago, and the wise man Chen who was a magistrate there:

The thief who kept his hands clean

Long years ago in south China there lived a magistrate called Chen whose wisdom equalled his love of justice. He was admired and revered by all the honest people under his rule.

One night there was a great robbery in the district. The constable, eager to win the admiration of Magistrate Chen, quickly swept up every possible suspect in the neighbourhood and crammed the lot of them into the courtroom. He then set himself to questioning each in turn, asking the whereabouts and the wherefores and the whens and whats, until he had amassed so many twists of fact that he was quite entangled in them. At last he had to admit defeat and, as on many another occasion, he turned the hopeless jumble over to the magistrate.

At the preliminary hearing, Magistrate Chen heard the charges, but instead of questioning the suspects, he announced, "Upon the eastern hill in the Temple of the Great Buddha there is an old bronze bell which will tell us who the robber is."

Thereupon he sent the constable's men to transport the bell from the temple to the court, and gave orders for a blue cotton canopy to be spread on poles above it. The night before the trial he himself set firepots in the four quarters round the bell and lit them. When the fires finally died away, he slowly lowered the blue canopy until the bell was completely hidden in its folds.

Because Magistrate Chen's judgements were famous, people thronged to the courtroom the next day to attend the trial. There was scarcely room for them and all the suspects too.

Without preamble the magistrate addressed the suspects. "This old bronze bell from the Temple of the Great Buddha has powers of divination beyond those of man or magistrate," he said. "Ten thousand innocent people may rub it and no sound will be heard, but let one thief touch his hand to its side, and a clear peal will sound out his guilt for all the world to hear." He paused and looked intently at the suspects. "In a few moments I shall ask each of you to put his hand under the blue cover and rub the bell."

Solemnly, the magistrate bowed his head and made a prayer in front of the bell. Then, one by one, he led the suspects forward and watched while they put their hands under the cover to rub the bell. As each suspect turned away without the bell's having sounded, the crowd gave a little sigh, but when the last man had passed the test, there was a restless stirring. The bell had failed!

But the magistrate clapped his hand on the shoulder of the last suspect.

"Here is the thief we are looking for," he declared.

A stir of outrage spread over the crowd.

The accused spluttered. "Your Honour! When I rubbed the bell, there was no more sound than when all the others did the same thing! How can you so unjustly accuse me!"

"He's right!" somebody in the crowd shouted.

Indignant cries rang out on all sides.

"Unfair!" "Injustice!"

The magistrate, unperturbed, gave his beard a tidy stroke. "Remove the cover," he said to the constable.

The constable did his bidding.

There was a gasp of amazement round the

courtroom, and then the crowd fell silent as they began to understand what had passed. The gleaming bell they had seen brought to the court was now black with soot — save round the rim where many innocent hands had rubbed through the grime to the gleaming bronze.

"Truly this old bell has powers of divination," Magistrate Chen said, "Truly, it uttered no sound when innocent people rubbed it. And it uttered no sound when the thief put his hand under the cover, for only the thief was afraid to rub the bell for fear of its revealing peal. Therefore, only the thief brought his hand out from under the cover free of soot."

All eyes came to focus on the shamefully clean hands of the thief, and a murmur of admiration swelled from the crowd.

Truly it was a magic bell. And Magistrate Chen was something of a magician.

Oral tradition.

2. HOLI

Hindu festival of spring

Holi is celebrated during the harvest of wheat and mustard throughout India. It is in late February or early March. A large bonfire made from sticks is burned the night before: The burning of Holika. We would put pinenuts in the kernels, chick peas on stalks into the fire to roast, then pull them out quickly and eat them — almost burning our mouths and fingers! The next day is Holi. It is also called the Festival of Colour. There are buckets full of brightly coloured water. With long syringes we could drench friends and foes with Holi. On this day it does not matter which caste or creed you belong to. Everyone is free to play Holi with anyone. Colours like yellow, red, orange and green are used in powder or paint form. Some even go to the extent of revengeful black and purple. Its fun to play Holi with members of the opposite sex which would normally be a taboo. As usual delicious foods and sweets are prepared. People wear old clothes all day to play Holi, then get washed and changed in the evening.

Kavita Sharma.

Throwing coloured water is a fun custom deriving from playful stories of Krishna and Radha who splashed each other on the river Yamura when enjoying fresh spring weather. In the classroom or community hall, coloured confetti paper is a good substitute!

The Holi eve bonfire celebrates the victory of good over evil:

The saving of Prahlad

In ancient times there lived a powerful ruler named King Hiranyakashup. The King saw himself as a god-like figure and commanded all to worship him. But his own son Prahlad refused, believing instead that worship should be directed to God, to Vishnu.

King Hiranyakashup was furious when his son declared his own belief and in his fury declared he would see the young prince killed. He ordered his soldiers to throw Prahlad into a deep pit full of poisonous snakes where he was bitten but miraculously survived. Then the king ordered that a herd of elephants be stampeded to trample over the prince as he slept. But God protected Prahlad from harm and again he escaped death. Some say the elephants themselves refused to harm him!.

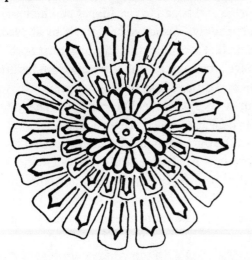

Each time the King commanded a new death plot, he failed. Finally he turned to his wicked sister, Holika. Now Holika had a special quality of strength which meant that fire could not harm her. She was known throughout the Kingdom as one who would not burn — neither candles, cooking fires nor open flames held fear for her. Fiercely she took Prahlad to the top of a huge bonfire so that he would be burnt to death.

The flames leapt about them but God made his final sign: Prahlad stepped from the fire unharmed while the spell protecting the wicked Holika was broken and it was she who disappeared. In this way heavenly goodness won over earthly evil, and this story is remembered by lighting a bonfire and watching the sparks and embers every year.

Remembering the birth of Lord Krishna

Krishna is one of the two most famous human forms of the god Vishnu, who is one of the three most important Hindu gods. The other form is Rama, whose story is told later in this book.

Long ago, there was a wicked king called Kansa, who was told by his sages that one day he would be killed by the eighth child born to his sister, Devaki.

Kansa was terrified and enraged. He decided to kill every child that Devaki had. He plotted to keep a guard on Devaki and her husband, Vasudeva. He had them watched night and day so that the minute a baby was born it would be destroyed.

Kansa wanted to keep his evil plan a secret. He made his guards swear not to tell anyone. "I don't want the gods to hear about it," he said.

But the gods did hear about it. Lord Vishnu, the preserver, god of goodness and mercy, heard about it. Vishnu has the power to be born again many times and in many different ways.

He decided to be reborn as Devaki's eighth child. "I will be the one to destroy King Kansa," he said.

When Devaki's eighth child was due to be born, Kansa had her and Vasudeva imprisoned. They were chained to the walls, and guards sat night and day at the door. Vasudeva clenched his fist with anguish. How could he save their baby?

It was the very middle of the night and a strange calm hung over the world. A full moon floated majestically over a trembling earth. There was not even a breath of a wind to stir the dusty ground.

Suddenly, the moment arrived. Devaki's eighth child was born. As the dark, moist body of a boy wriggled into the world, a shiver of excitement vibrated round the universe. Up in heaven the drums thudded wildly. Lord Indra sent a shower or flowers and raindrops tumbling down out of the sky. All the devas and apsaras, the nymphs and the rishis burst into song. "Lord Vishnu is reborn as a man, and his name is Krishna!"

Vasudeva held his son fearfully. Everyone was asleep. The women who should have helped with the birth were snoring in a corner. Outside the prison door, the guards were slumped on the floor.

Suddenly the baby opened his eyes. It was like the windows of heaven opening. Devaki and Vasudeva found the chains had fallen from their bodies, and the locks on the door flew open.

"Quick! Escape! Save our baby!" cried Devaki.

Vasudeva gathered up baby Krishna. "I'll take him somewhere safe," he whispered.

With tears streaming down her face, Devaki kissed her child, then Vasudeva crept out into the night.

On the other side of the River Yamuna lived a cowherd and his wife called Nanda and Yasoda. They were good, honest people, and Vasudeva knew he could trust them. He hurried down to the river banks and, holding his baby close, began to wade across.

Suddenly, a storm blew up. The waters swirled and began to rise higher and higher. Desperately, Vasudeva held the baby above his head. Just when he thought they must both drown, the baby Krishna stretched out his little foot and dipped it in the angry waters. Immediately the river became calm. The waters fell and Vasudeva could get across.

In the dark of night, Vasudeva handed his precious son to Nanda and Yasoda. They looked on the beautiful boy and loved him as their own child.

So Krishna went to live among the cowherds. He seemed such a normal, human boy. He played all day with the village children, and he was so naughty!

"Krishna! Krishna!" How that name rang out across the fields! "Krishna is a naughty boy!" came the shout, but it was never in anger. No one could be cross with him for long. Even though he liked hanging on to cows' tails and being dragged across meadows. Even though he teased the milkmaids and stole their milk and butter. Krishna had only to flash his black eyes, or laugh and show his rows of little pearly teeth, and all was forgiven.

Yasoda would watch the boy and sometimes feel a pang of fear, as all mothers do. She knew what dreadful dangers lurked for a naughty, active boy. She feared the demon ogress who liked eating children. She feared the serpent who lay in wait by the river.

One day the village children rushed up to Yasoda.

"Krishna's naughty! He's eating chalk!" they cried.

Yasoda jumped up angrily and ran to the boy.

"What's all this I hear? Have you been eating chalk?" she cried. She was angry because she was so worried.

"No, I haven't," said Krishna. "The children are lying to get me into trouble."

"Open your mouth then!" snapped Yasoda.

Krishna opened his mouth wide. Yasoda looked. Time and space stood still. Yasoda found herself gazing into the mouth of eternity. She saw all heaven and earth; the mountain ranges and rushing rivers. She saw the jungles and deserts and she even saw her own little village with the herdsmen in the fields. She saw the planets of the zodiac and the galaxies of the universe. She saw earth, water, fire and air. Yasoda gazed at creation itself in the mouth of Lord Vishnu.

In that moment, she understood. She knew that she did not need to protect Krishna. He would protect her.

When Krishna shut his mouth, Yasoda immediately forgot what she had seen. But her heart overflowed with love for him. She took him on her lap, and she knew she would never be afraid again.

Jamila Gavin.

Raita

Raita is a light savoury yoghurt dish that is the perfect accompaniment to any spicy dish, or even with cold pies and salads.

Cucumber raita:

1 cucumber
3 cups (675ml) yoghurt
1 teaspoon cumin seed or chopped mint, dill or
    fennel
1 teaspoon salt
Dash of cayenne pepper

Peel, seed and coarsely grate or finely chop the cucumber. Roast the cumin seeds in a heavy pan for several minutes before grinding them and combining them with the yoghurt, cucumber and other ingredients. Chill well and garnish with mint leaves before serving.

Banana raita:

2 ripe bananas
3 cups (675ml) yoghurt
Dash of cayenne pepper
Dash of cinnamon
Dash of cardamom
1 teaspoon fresh lemon juice

Mash one of the bananas well with some of the yoghurt. Chop the other into 1cm (½") chunks. Combine all the ingredients and chill well.

Samosas

Samosas are delicious Indian savouries. They are small packets of pastry filled with tasty spicy vegetables and deep fried.

Filling:

2 large potatoes, cooked and mashed
1 finely chopped small onion
2 medium cloves garlic, crushed
½ teaspoon ginger — fresh if possible
½ teaspoon mustard seeds
½ teaspoon ground coriander
2 medium carrots, cooked and diced
½ cup (approx 75g) cooked green peas
1 teaspoon salt
Pinch cayenne pepper
Juice of ½ lemon
2 – 3 tablespoons butter

Pastry:

2 cups (400g) white flour
1 teaspoon salt
4 tablespoons melted butter
⅓ cup (75ml) plain yoghurt
Water to bind

To make the filling, heat the butter in a heavy frying pan and sauté the onion with the garlic, ginger, mustard seeds and salt, until the onion is soft and clear. Combine all the ingredients in a bowl, mixing well. Add the peas last so that they remain whole.

To make the pastry, sift the flour and salt together. Add the melted butter, yoghurt and enough water to make a stiff dough. Knead until smooth and elastic and roll the pastry out very thinly on a floured board. Cut into circles 10cm (4″) in diameter.

Place a spoonful of filling in the centre of each circle. Brush the edges with water and fold one side over the other to make a little parcel. Press down and seal with a fork.

Heat about 5cm (3″) of sunflower or peanut oil in a heavy pan until it is beginning to smoke. Fry the samosas until golden. Drain on absorbent paper and serve hot.

3. EID-UL-FITR

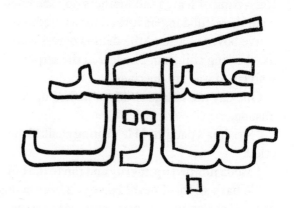

Eid-ul-fitr

The religion Islam stems from the Middle East and had spread to East Asia, India and Pakistan when trading routes first opened.

The religion has five pillars:

1. First and foremost the belief in one god Allah.
2. Prayers, Namaz to be performed five times a day.
3. Pilgrimage to Mecca.
4. Charity, Zakat.
5. Fasting for a month in the month of Ramadan.

The month in which the fasting is observed is called Ramadan, the ninth month of the Islamic calender. The fast begins before dawn and is broken at dusk. All new months begin with the sighting of the moon, the new moon on the last

RAMADAN IS COME

Traditional

Wa - ha - wi ya wa - ha - wi ee yo _____ ha.
Ra - ma - dan ___ Ra - ma - dan Ra - ma - dan is come.

Wahawi ya wahawi ee yo ha.
Bintill Sultan ee yo ha.
Labsa koftan ee yo ha.
Bilah mari ee yo ha.
Bilas faril ee yo ha.
Bilakh dari ee yo ha.
Wahawi ya wahawi ee yo ha.

Ramadan, Ramadan, Ramadan is come.
The sultan's daughter, ee yo ha.
In a kaftan garbed, ee yo ha.
Of rose-red hue, ee yo ha.
Or in sunlight gold, ee yo ha.
Or a green so bright, ee yo ha.
Ramadan, Ramadan, Ramadan is come.

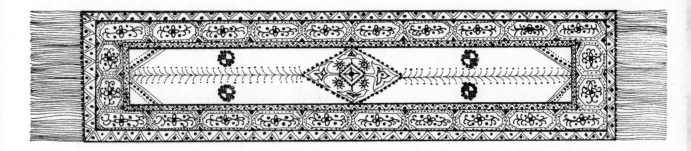

day being the evening of the 29th day will mean that the Eid celebrations can begin but if there is no moon on the 29th day then an extra fast has to be kept.

As a child on the 9th evening of fasting I would be wishing that God would send down the moon, so that I would not have to keep another fast. I can eat and drink all the time till the following Ramadan. The anticipation of not knowing (as sometimes it can get very late in the night for news of the moon to come) would make me very excited! The male members would have all gone to the Mosque to find out if the moon had been sighted.

My new clothes from underwear to ornaments would be ready and would have been displayed on the chair. So my mum would not have to hunt for them the next day. I know now why my mum would not be very happy if the moon would come on the 29th day as she would be very busy with all the preparations that have been going on several days before Eid. It is a custom to stock up on sweet dishes, halva, cakes, biscuits which sometimes meant work for me too.

On Eid day mum would have got up early for morning prayers. She would have already bathed and made a pot of sweet almond milk which is a traditional drink made in most houses. She would wake me up and first, give me a bath as the night before I would have had mehndi on my hands and feet. Then and only then could I put on my new clothes. When my father, who had been up early and gone to Mosque for special Eid Namaz came home, we would all shake hands, all the members of the family would visit us and mum would hand round the special sweet milk and a few of the sweet meats.

Lots of relatives and friends visit each other, the morning in our house was spent welcoming everyone. By about 11 o'clock mum's cooking would have come to an end and she would have cooked lots of savoury dishes for the Eid day meal. Even though I would not be fasting I would not eat anything in case my clothes were to get dirty. I couldn't wait for the meal to be over so that the time to give presents and money would come round. My parents always gave me and my brothers and sisters the same amount of money so we wouldn't fight.

In the afternoon I would go to my friends' and relatives' houses and talk about how much money or what presents I might have had. Sometimes photographs would be taken so that we could send them back home to our grandparents as it was one of the very rare times families would be all together. Depending on what time of year it was I would sometimes be taken out to visit a park by a grown up, as it could get boring when the grown ups got together.

The Eid celebrations can go on for three days but most people in this country only take a day's holiday as they do not have a paid holiday.

Gori Nanabawa.

How to make a Mehndi design

Mehndi powder or henna is made from the crushed dried leaves of the mehndi plant.

Some Asian women and girls use mehndi powder to decorate their hands for festival occasions.

Brides also decorate their hands and feet with beautiful mendhi designs for their wedding day.

Mehndi powder should be used carefully because it can stain clothing and carpets.

Materials required:

Mehndi powder
Water
Lemon juice
Spent matchstick, cocktail stick

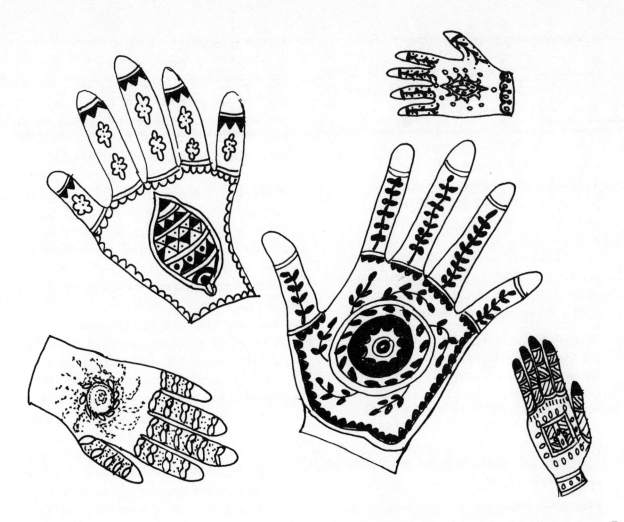

Method

1. Put a small quantity of mehndi powder into a saucer (dish).
2. Add a few drops of lemon juice and enough warm water to make a paste.
3. Apply the paste with the matchstick to the palms of the hands. More delicate patterns can be made with a cocktail stick.
4. Leave the paste design to dry, then wash off.
5. A bright orange/brown pigment will be left on the skin. The longer the paste is left on the hand, the longer the design will remain after washing and the deeper the colour.
6. Rub lemon juice onto the designs to help to prevent them from fading too quickly.

If it is preferable not to stain the hands, mehndi designs can be produced using an orange/brown or red felt pen on outline drawings of the hand.

Shortcake biscuit hands:

Younger children will enjoy making decorated biscuit shaped hands. The following recipe is simple enough for children to follow if the dough is made by an adult and is rolled into balls. The young child's main pleasure will be concentrated on tracing and baking their own hand shapes and decorating them with sweets, nuts or glacé icing when cold. Split blanched almonds make excellent fingernails.

Small children must not be allowed to touch the oven. Baking should be put into the oven and later removed by an adult.

200g (½ cup) soft margarine
50g (2oz) sifted icing sugar
150g (⅝) sifted plain flour
125g (½ cup) sifted self-raising flour
1 tablespoon cornflour

Beat margarine in a bowl. Add the icing sugar and continue beating the mixture until light and fluffy. Work in the flours and cornflour. Knead lightly to make a smooth dough.

Wrap the dough in tin foil and chill in the fridge for 30 minutes. Heat the oven to 350°F, 180°C, gas mark 4.

Lightly flour the pastry board and roll out dough to 6mm (¼″) thick. Place a hand on the dough and trace round it with a cutting wheel. Place on a baking tray and cook for 15 minutes or until light brown.

Cool for a minute then transfer to a wire rack. Decorate hands when cold.

Glacé icing can be used in a piping bag to produce a mehndi design. Young children will enjoy making random patterns with sweets or icing.

Glacé icing:

50g (2oz) sifted icing sugar
½ – 1 tablespoon of lemon juice or warm water
A few drops of orange or red food colouring will represent the sacred colours.

A fond memory...

Yes, I used to love the mosque, and I loved the river too. Directly we finished our Koran reading in the morning I would throw down my wooden slate and dart off, quick as a genie, to my mother, hurriedly swallow down my breakfast, and run off for a plunge in the river. When tired of swimming about I would sit on the bank and gaze at the strip of water that wound away eastwards and hid behind a thick wood of acacia trees. I loved to give rein to my imagination and picture to myself a tribe of giants living behind that wood, a people tall and thin with white beards and sharp noses, like my grandfather. Before my grandfather ever replied to my many questions he would rub the tip of his nose with his forefinger; as for his beard, it was soft and luxuriant and as white as cotton wool — never in my life have I seen anything of a purer whiteness or greater beauty. My grandfather must also have been extremely tall, for I never saw anyone in the whole area address him without having to look up at him, nor did I see him enter a house without having to bend so low that I was put in mind of the way the river wound round behind the wood of acacia trees. I loved him and would imagine myself, when I grew to be a man, tall and slender like him, walking along with great strides.

Tayeb Salih from "A Handful of Dates"
in *The Wedding of Zein.*

Mosque collage

Make a collage or mosaic of a mosque:

Use scraps of tissue, card, silver foil and gold paper; pebbles; broken china; sweet wrappers; leaves… and anything else to create colourful shapes and patterns.

Abd al-Muttalib and the well of Zam-Zam

Late one night, long ago, an aged Arabic chief told this story to his little grandson, Muhammad. It all took place in Makka, an ancient city in the vast desert country of Arabia.

In Makka, there stands a sacred place called the Ka'ba. It has been sacred since the time of Abraham, perhaps even much earlier from the time of Adam. It was there, they say, that the Angel Gabriel presented the Prophet Abraham with a milk-white stone from Paradise. Since that time, the stone, according to the story, has been tarnished by the sins of man, and has turned black. So now it is called the Black Stone. Only a few pieces of it remain in the Ka'ba today, where Muslims from all over the world still come once a year on pilgrimage.

In the days of Abd al-Muttalib, Muhammad's grandfather, all kinds of other objects were heaped in the Ka'ba. There were strange, oddly-shaped idols hewn out of red sandstone and other images carved into the shapes of men or goddesses. There were magic statues called Hubal, Al-Lat, Al-'Uzza that were believed to have the power to make you rich, cure you of the plague, grant you a son, or bring you the princess of your dreams. Most of the pilgrims had forgotten about the One Almighty God, and had through the years become idolators, putting their faith and trust into a carved image made by man, rather than in the One God that created man in the first place.

They worshipped their odd-shaped images with sacrifices, strange rites and chants; and in the evenings, while squatting in front of the Ka'ba, they drank and gambled or threw arrows and darts trying to foretell the future, while the crowds of eager listeners would gather around the storytellers.

These storytellers, the poets of Arabia, could neither read nor write, but they had marvellous memories and would spin long tales in beautiful poetry all about the Jinns — the spirits of the desert as they described them, the Jinns who create mirages in order to trick the traveller into thinking there is cool water ahead... or who cause the sands to sing mysteriously at night, with a sound like distant laughter. The storytellers would tell tales of battles and lost loves, as well as give the latest news from far-away places. They had the power to twist the truth or ruin a man's whole life by a verse or clever piece of gossip. They were the newsmen of the desert.

Muhammad's grandfather Abd al-Muttalib was a chief and belonged to an important family called the Quraysh, descended from the Prophet Abraham. Aged and respected, he had his own place in the Ka'ba, in front of the Sacred Well. Beside him sat his little grandson Muhammad the orphan. Other members of the clan would waggle their beards in disapproval at the way Abd al-Muttalib spoiled his grandson.

"He is only six years old and instead of sending him off to bed, you allow him to stay up among adults into the dark hours of the night..."

Abd al-Muttalib felt it was no business of theirs; the boy had been left in his charge, after the death of his parents. So Muhammad, wrapped in his grandfather's great cloak, would listen half the night to the many stories old Abd al-Muttalib liked telling to the family and friends who gathered around. Usually Muhammad fell asleep when the words were too difficult to understand, but tonight he knew that the stories his grandfather was telling were meant for his ears, too. And so he listened, his deep round eyes fixed on his grandfather's weathered skin and white beard.

"Now, when I was young and poor, and looked down upon by the wealthy members of my clan, my little son and I had the hard task of going from well to well, collecting water for the many pilgrims who came as they still do, from far across the desert to worship at the Ka'ba. The wells around the Ka'ba were often empty or gave bad water. That was before the Sacred Well had been found. Now — before I go on — do you remember the story of this well — the sacred well of Zam-Zam?"

Muhammad smiled in response — he certainly did remember it. But Abd al-Muttalib continued anyway, because he loved to tell the story.

"Hagar and her little son Ishmael, the son of Abraham, were brought to live in the valley of Makka, where there was no water and nothing grew. Soon they were wandering hopelessly under the hot desert sun. But it was not God's will that they should perish. Lo! The Angel Gabriel appeared in a vision of light. He struck the sand and up gushed a crystal-clear spring of water right at the little boy's feet. That spring was named the well of Zam-Zam. But in the course of time the well disappeared, and no one even knew where it had once been. Well now, my little son had heard the story as often as you have, and one day he asked me, 'Father, would a spring of water brought forth by the Angel Gabriel dry up and disappear forever?'

"I answered that if it was a sacred well, it certainly should not dry up. Then he asked me, 'If that were so, then, Father, where is it now?'

"Ah! That is what started us looking. We began digging and we dug for days and weeks. The winds kept shifting and the heavy sand filled in the holes we were digging again and again. Still we kept on and on, even though people — and members of my own clan — shrugged their shoulders in disgust or called out mockingly, 'You are looking for a needle in a sandstorm!' But you see, I was convinced. I was so sure we would find the well that I made a promise to myself and to God:

"If the sacred well of Zam-Zam is found, there will be no more laughter, there will be praise: and my name will be spoken with respect by the people of Makka and by my clan the Quraysh. Therfore, if I am blessed with ten sons, the tenth shall I offer up to the Almighty God.

"And then a remarkable thing happened. My spade struck something hard, and I unearthed two huge pieces of gold in the shape of gazelles. Right underneath where they had lain the sand was dark and moist — and the waters of Zam-Zam rose before our very eyes and filled the hole where the gazelles had been. Of course, some people were more interested in the gold than in the well, but I told them that the gold belonged to the Ka'ba, and if you look when you leave, you will see, Muhammad, the two gold disks hanging over the entry of the Ka'ba. From that day on the sweet waters of Zam-Zam have gushed forth generously for the pilgrims. And you see that your grandfather is praised and respected!"

At this the others smiled and nodded.

"And I was given a title: Keeper of the well of Zam-Zam, and my place is not out there, under the hot sun, but here in the shade of the Ka'ba, by the Sacred Well."

Mardijah A Tarantino,
Marvellous Stories from the Life of Muhammad.

4. PURIM

The Jewish festival of Lots — 14th Adar

Purim is a Jewish festival, which is also known as the Feast of Lots because Haman drew lots to establish the day on which to kill all Jews.

This traditional festival takes place each year during February/March, exactly four weeks before passover.

Purim is celebrated by reading from the scroll the Megillah, the book of Esther. Special Purim prayers are also said. It is significant that the book of Esther is one of only two books in the Bible which are named after women.

Queen Esther saved the Jews, living in the Persian Empire, from annihilation at the hand of the king's vizier, a wicked man called Haman. During the story, every time the villain Haman's name is mentioned, the children delight in making as much noise as possible to blot out his name. They stamp, hiss, blow whistles, shake rattles (greggors) and shout "May his name be blotted out".

After the service there is often a fancy dress parade or a party at which the children dress up or wear masks.

A special tea is eaten with three cornered Purim cakes called 'Haman's purse' (Haman-taschen) and 'Haman's ears' (Oznei Haman) (sugared fritters) on the menu.

In the book of Esther Jews are commanded to celebrate the custom of Purim each year with joy and feasting. It's also a day for giving gifts to each other and to those who are in need, ill or too elderly to leave their home.

The story of Queen Esther

A long time ago in the land called Persia, there lived a king named Xerxes (also known as Ahasuerus).

The King's wife, Queen Vashti, disobeyed him and made him look foolish in front of several lords and princes. The king was so angry that he vanquished Queen Vashti as a punishment and a warning to other wives and he began to look for another wife.

A beautiful and lovely girl named Esther was chosen to be Queen. She was the cousin of a Jewish man called Mordecai. When Mordecai instructed Esther not to tell anyone anything about her background or that she was a Jew, Esther did as she was told and kept the secret.

One day, Mordecai was sitting by the gate when he overheard two of the guards plotting to kill the King. Mordecai immediately informed Queen Esther of the plot. Queen Esther warned her husband the King. The plot was thwarted and the whole event was written in the official records of the Persian Empire.

Not long after this incident a man called Haman became the vizier to King Xerxes. Now Haman was a conceited, pompous man who expected all the other minor (less important) officials and administrators to bow down to him whenever he passed by. Mordecai refused to honour Haman in this way because he was Jewish and would only bow down to God, not to a mere man.

This made Haman so furious that he decided to kill not just Mordecai but all Jewish people.

Haman cast the spur (that is the lot) to decide a date on which to carry out this evil deed. The date drawn was the 13th day of the 12th Jewish month known as Adar. This is in March in the Western calender.

When Mordecai and other Jews throughout Persia heard of Haman's cruel proclamation, which would mean death to Jewish men, women and children, they went into mourning and wore sack cloth instead of their usual clothing.

Mordecai begged Queen Esther to plead with the King to save the Jewish people. Esther was very hesitant because she knew that if she went to see the King without an invitation, she would be breaking a law and she could be killed. Esther was persuaded by Mordecai that if she didn't convince the King to spare the Jewish people, she too would be killed. After thinking about the situation Esther decided that she wanted to help to save her people. She asked Mordecai and some other Jews to pray and fast for her for three days and three nights. Esther also prayed and fasted and when the three days and nights had passed she dressed herself in her most beautiful clothes and went to the King's court.

King Xerxes was delighted to see Queen Esther and held out his golden sceptre to encourage her to enter his presence.

Queen Esther was told she could request up to half the Kingdom, but instead of accepting immediately, she had a plan. She invited King Xerxes and Haman to a special banquet to be held in their honour.

During the banquet the King asked Esther what she wanted, Esther remained silent and did not disclose the reason for her visit to the King and instead invited the King and Haman to a second banquet the following evening.

Haman was so pleased with himself as he went home that night even though Mordecai did not bow to him as he left the King's gate. When he arrived home he boasted to his family and friends about his importance with the King, Queen and Mordecai and also mentioned the special invitation for the following night. However, he grumbled that Mordecai's lack of respect still made him furious. Upon hearing

this his family suggested that he should build some very high gallows near his home, to hang Mordecai on. Haman thought that this was a good idea and ordered the gallows to be built.

That night after the first banquet, the King could not sleep so he demanded that the official records of his reign be brought into his room and read to him. The record of Mordecai's action in saving the King's life was read out. The King asked what reward Mordecai had received. When the King was told that no reward had been given to Mordecai, he racked his brains to think of a suitable award to honour Mordecai.

Nothing suitable came to mind so the next day the King asked Haman how he could honour a special man. Conceited Haman thought that he was the man the King wished to honour. He therefore suggested the man should be dressed in royal robes, mounted on a royal horse and led by noblemen through the city. Haman suggested that noblemen should announce that this is what is done for the man the King delights to honour.

The King was thrilled with Haman's idea and he insisted that Haman went immediately and carried out his suggestion to honour Mordecai.

Haman was so ashamed to have to parade the honoured Mordecai through the streets and was mortified when his family and friends suggested that Mordecai was replacing him in the King's favour.

Later that night when Haman dined with the King and Queen, Esther made her request that she and her people be saved from death. She informed the King of the plan to annihilate them. The King was furious and demanded to know who was behind the vile plot. Esther told him that it was Haman. The angry King went out into the garden to consider the situation. In his absence Haman threw himself at Queen Esther's feet in order to plead for his life. Esther was reclining on a couch; and when the King returned he saw Haman grovelling at Esther's feet, he presumed that he was trying to seduce her and ordered Haman's immediate death.

Haman was hanged on the gallows he had prepared for Mordecai. The King immediately elevated Mordecai into a high position and gave him the signet ring which he had reclaimed from Haman.

Mordecai recorded all these events then he wrote to the Jews throughout King Xerxes' Province to tell them to celebrate with feasting and joy every year on the 14th and 15th day of Adar.

From the Book of Esther in the *Old Testament*.

Make your own Megillah

Use a long piece of paper or glue sheets of A4 paper together to make your Megillah. Write out the story of Purim and draw and colour pictures of the main characters.

Remember, Jews read the scroll from right to left!

Start writing here.

Roll this way.

Glue this end round an empty kitchen roll tube.

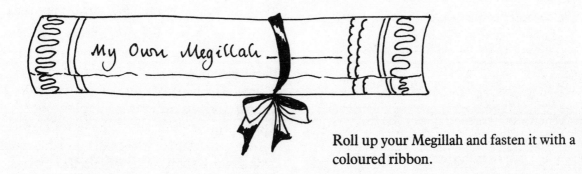

My Own Megillah

Roll up your Megillah and fasten it with a coloured ribbon.

To make a greggor

Greggors are shaken vigorously to blot out the name of Haman during the re-telling of the story.

Use an empty fizzy drink can. Cut a circle of stiff card to cover the ring pull end of the can. Before gluing the card in place put dried beans, pasta shells or small pebbles into the can. Cover the outside of the can with a plain paper and decorate. Enjoy shaking your greggor!

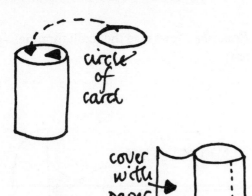

A song for Purim

To the tune of "If you're happy and you know it."

1. When you hear the name of Haman,
   stamp your feet!
2. When you hear the name of Esther,
   shout "Hurray!"
3. When you hear the name of Xerxes,
   wave your arms!
4. When you hear the name of Mordecai,
   bow your head!

Hamantchen (Haman's purses)

1½ cups (300g) flour
2 teaspoons baking powder
⅝ cup (125g) sugar
125g margarine
2 eggs
1 teaspoon vanilla essence

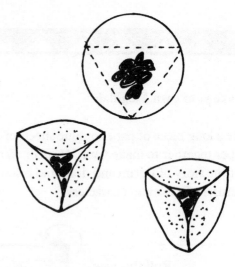

Mix the dry ingredients. Cut in margarine. Add beaten eggs and vanilla essence. Mix dough until it forms a ball. Roll out thinly on a floured board. Cut into 3″ (7.5cm) circles using a cutter or the rim of a drinking glass. Place a spoonful of filling in the centre, then draw up three sides to form a triangle, and pinch edges firmly together. Brush the tops with a little beaten egg. Bake in a moderate oven, 350°F, 180°C, Gas Mark 4, for 25 – 30 minutes. Makes approx 24.

Suggested fillings:

Vegetarian mincemeat
Stewed apple
Chocolate chips
Apricot jam

This recipe produces a cakey pastry. Ready made, frozen pastry could also be used.

Oznej Haman (Haman's ears)

1 cup (200g) plain flour
1 teaspoon baking powder
¼ cup (25g) caster sugar
2 eggs
½ teaspoon salt
1 tablespoon water

Beat the eggs until fluffy, then add the salt, sugar and water beating well. Stir in the flour to make a soft-but-not-sticky dough. Roll out thinly on a floured board. Cut into half moons using a 2″ (5cm) cutter or the rim of a drinking glass, moving the cutter down the dough to form crescents. Pinch each crescent in the centre so that it looks like a bow tie with an 'ear' on either side of the centre. Fry the 'ears' until golden brown, drain on kitchen paper. Serve hot or cold after sprinkling with icing sugar.

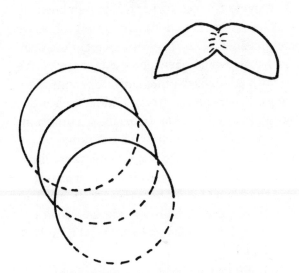

Falafel

A very popular snack in the Middle East, Falafel is now also enjoyed in cities all over Europe.

2 cups (400g) chick peas
2 small onions, grated
2 – 3 cloves garlic, crushed
Bunch of parsley, finely chopped
Pinch of salt and cayenne pepper
2 teaspoons ground cumin
2 teaspoons ground coriander
Oil for frying

Cook the chickpeas until soft. Put them, with all the other ingredients, through a fine mincer or mouli. Then mix well and pound to a smooth paste. Or you can simply liquidise the whole mixture.

Leave the chick pea paste to stand for an hour, then take small lumps and make flattened balls about 4cm (1½″) in diameter. Fry them in hot oil until they are a dark golden brown on both sides.

Falafel are delicious eaten with salad and pitta bread, or served with tahini dressing, rice and salad.

Crowns and masks

The story of Purim can be acted out when the children read from their Megillah.

The children can make simple crowns from cardboard and decorate them with coloured foil and fabric.

The ends can be stapled together to fit the child's head.

Another method of dramatising the story is by using masks. Masks can be made quite easily by young children using either large paper plates or the cardboard from a cereal packet. Cut out the eyes and decorate the face with hair, crown, eyebrows, moustache, beard or hat. Staple a strip of card to each side of the mask to fit around the head.

More elaborate masks can be made from papier-mâché and attached to sticks. These masks are held in front of the child's face. Older children can write their own scripts while younger ones will enjoy miming to the story.

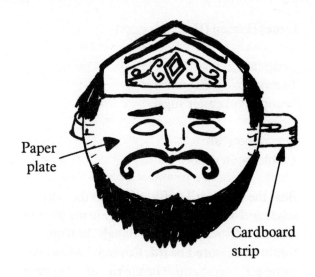

Paper plate

Cardboard strip

5. St DAVID'S DAY

St David's Day — 1st March

When I was a little girl, living by the sea in South Wales, I looked forward each year to Saint David's Day or Dydd Gwyl Dewi as it is known in Welsh.

I would get up early, as getting dressed in my Welsh costume took some time. First underclothes including a 'paish' or petticoat with a white vest top and a skirt of red Welsh flannel. Then the 'betcwm' a little like a dress with a slit at the front. The two front ends were fastened back so the paish could be seen. The betcwm was of red and black check. Over all went a black and white check apron — also flannel and a paisley shawl. On our heads we wore either the tall black straight-sided hat with the wide brim or the 'cockle hats' like bonnets. We then put on our daffodils and feeling very proud, if a bit prickly, we set off to school.

Boys did not have a national costume but they sported Wales's other national emblem — leeks, somtimes of enormous size. At school we congregated for the biggest concert of the year. Each class would have rehearsed for weeks. We performed for each other and our parents the songs, dances and poetry of Wales. We heard through song, dance or drama the story of Saint David, how he cured the sick and through prayer could make wells spring up where they were needed. The concert lasted all morning and the smell of leeks became very strong. The morning ended with groups of us going with bunches of daffodils to past staff and friends of the school.

The afternoon was free and most years I, like most of my friends, went to the photographer — few families had cameras — for an annual photograph given and sent to relatives who told me I'd grown! In the evening we repeated the concert at the local chapel for the whole community to enjoy a nostalgic, thoroughly

Welsh evening.

Even at my more English orientated Grammar School, Dydd Gwyl Dewi was special. We held an Eisteddfod — Eisteddfodau are competitive festivals held throughout the year in the towns and villages of Wales. Every girl in the school had to compete in as many events as possible to gain glory for her 'house' or team. All talents were fostered as songs, prose and poems were learnt and delivered in French, German, Latin and English as well as Welsh. There were music competitions from solos to choirs and violins to ensembles. We wrote limericks, sonnets, essays and bardic poetry. The Eisteddfod took a day and a half and all contributed, so the feeling of tension and relief, of anticipation and achievement all combined to make Dydd Gwyl Dewi a highlight of the year, a day that dispelled winter and heralded spring.

Ann Lewis.

SPRING SONG

Jehanne Mehta

1. Wake up, wake up all you lit-tle chil-dren, Sun-light, sky-bright, spring is co-ming now. Gus-ty March winds blow-ing Daf-fo-dils a-bow-ing Birds sing, bells ring, there's blos-som on the bough.

2. Piper, piper, play your happy music;
   Singing, singing, we will follow on.
   Dancing through the day time,
   Lead us to the May time.
   Ding dong, spring song, the winter's past and gone.

59

6. APRIL FOOLS DAY

April fools day

The first day of April is known as a time for practical jokes and fooling. The spirit of general jesting seems to come from ancient times and a need for something mischievous or comical to challenge order and convention. In the Roman empire, for example, a slave or servant was made ruler for the day during the feast of Saturnalia. In some European courts the jester had his day in seeing 'misrule' and pranks.

Today the day is an excuse for small pranks — until Midday, that is. If you play a trick after this you are a fool yourself! Salt in the sugar bowl, mis-matched shoes or unlikely pronouncements ("Mrs Smith the neighbour had triplets last night!") are to be watched for! It should of course be good natured — I was reduced to fits of laughter once by a beautifully wrapped bouquet of completely wilted daffodils.

For smaller children in the classroom, why not give over a few minutes to celebrate the improbable?

April rain song

Let the rain kiss you.
Let the rain beat upon your head with
*   silver liquid drops.*
Let the rain sing you a lullaby.

The rain makes still ponds on the sidewalk.
The rain makes running pools in the gutter.
The rain plays a little sleep song on our
*   roof at night —*

And I love the rain.

Langston Hughes.

I saw an ape thatching a barn,
And a frog wind balls of yarn,
And a codfish sowing corn.

I saw a hedgehog cut and sew
And a worm a whistle blow.
And a Kipper bend a bow.

I saw a pudding eat a pie,
And a sow hang out her washing to dry.
It isn't long since I told a lie!

Anon.

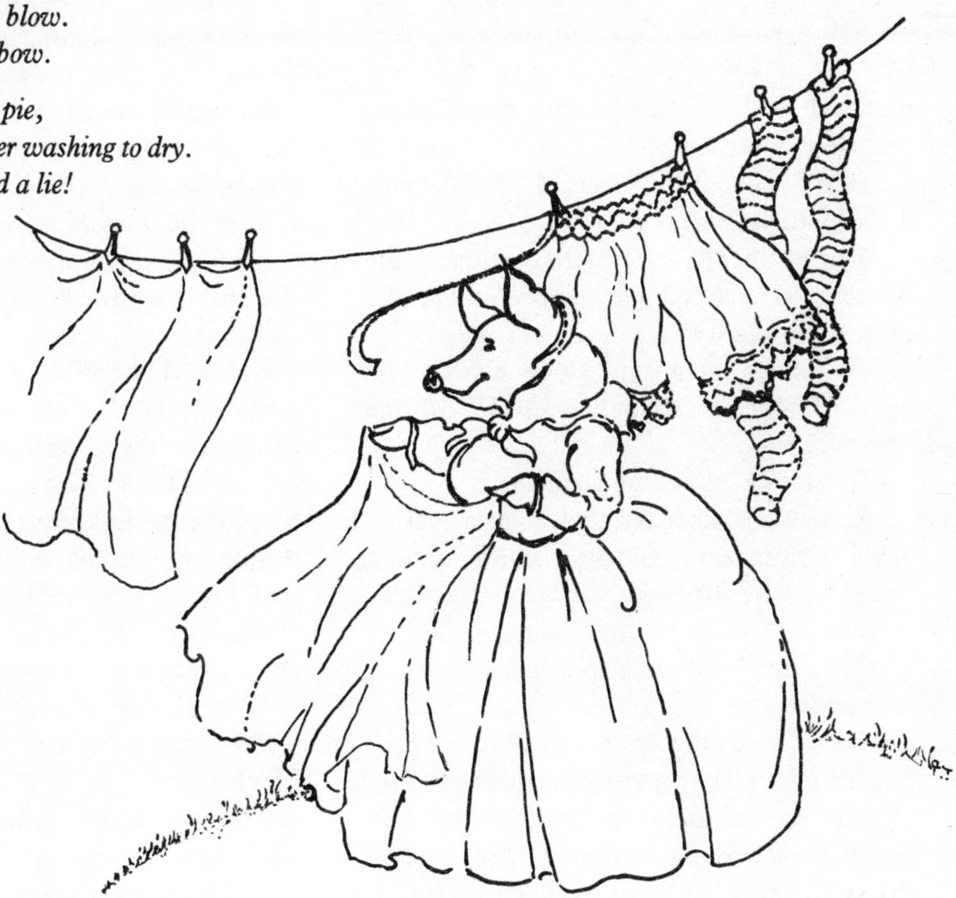

The whale and the elephant

One day little Brother Rabbit was running along on the sand, lippety, lippety, when he saw the Whale and the Elephant talking together. Little Brother Rabbit crouched down and listened to what they were saying. This was what they were saying:

"You are the biggest thing on the land, Brother Elephant," said the Whale, "and I am the biggest thing in the sea; if we join together we can rule all the animals in the world, and have our way about everything."

"Very good, very good," trumpeted the Elephant; "that suits me; we will do it."

Little Brother Rabbit sniggered to himself. "They won't rule me," he said. He ran away and got a very long, very strong rope, and he got his big drum, and hid the drum a long way off in the bushes. Then he went along the beach till he came to the Whale.

"Oh, please, dear, strong Mr Whale," he said, "will you have the great kindness to do me a favour? My cow is stuck in the mud, a quarter of a mile from here. And I can't pull her out. But you are so strong and so obliging, that I

61

venture to trust you will help me out."

The Whale was so pleased with the compliment that he said, "Yes," at once.

"Then," said the Rabbit, "I will tie this end of my long rope to you, and I will run away and tie the other end round my cow, and when I am ready I will beat my big drum. When you hear that, pull very, very hard, for the cow is stuck very deep in the mud."

"Huh!" grunted the Whale, "I'll pull her out, if she is stuck to the horns."

Little Brother Rabbit tied the rope-end to the Whale, and ran off, lippety, lippety, till he came to the place where the Elephant was.

"Oh, please, mighty and kindly Elephant," he said, making a very low bow, "will you do me a favour?"

"What is it?" asked the Elephant.

"My cow is stuck in the mud, about a quarter of a mile from here," said little Brother Rabbit, "and I cannot pull her out. Of course you could. If you will be so very obliging as to help me..."

"Certainly," said the Elephant grandly, "certainly."

"Then," said little Brother Rabbit, "I will tie one end of this long rope to your trunk, and the other to my cow, and as soon as I have tied her tightly I will beat my big drum. When you hear that, pull; pull as hard as you can, for my cow is very heavy."

"Never fear," said the Elephant, "I could pull twenty cows."

"I am sure you could," said the Rabbit, politely, "only be sure to begin gently, and pull harder and harder till you get her."

Then he tied the end of the rope tightly round the Elephant's trunk, and ran away into the bushes. There he sat down and beat the big drum.

The Whale began to pull, and the Elephant began to pull, and in a jiffy the rope tightened till it was stretched as hard as could be.

"This is a remarkably heavy cow," said the Elephant; "but I'll fetch her!" And he braced his forefeet in the earth, and gave a tremendous pull.

"Dear me!" said the Whale. "That cow must be stuck mighty tight"; and he drove his tail deep in the water, and gave a marvellous pull.

He pulled harder; the Elephant pulled harder. Pretty soon the Whale found himself sliding toward the land. The reason was, of course, that the Elephant had something solid to brace against, and, beside, as fast as he pulled the rope in a little, he took a turn with it round his trunk!

But when the Whale found himself sliding toward the land he was so provoked with the cow that he dived head first, down to the bottom of the sea. That was a pull! The Elephant was jerked off his feet, and came slipping and sliding to the beach, and into the surf. He was terribly angry. He braced himself with all his might, and pulled his best. At the jerk, up came the Whale out of the water.

"Who is pulling me?" spouted the Whale.

"Who is pulling me?" trumpeted the Elephant.

And then each saw the rope in the other's hold.

"I'll teach you to play cow!" roared the Elephant.

"I'll show you how to fool me!" fumed the Whale. And they began to pull again. But this time the rope broke, the Whale turned a somersault, and the Elephant fell over backward.

At that, they were both so ashamed that neither would speak to the other. So that broke up the bargain between them.

And little Brother Rabbit sat in the bushes and laughed, and laughed, and laughed.

7. EASTER

Easter Day

Easter Sunday is one of the most important Christian festivals as it celebrates the miracle of Jesus overcoming death. The previous Friday, traditionally held as Good Friday, is marked as the day he was crucified. The festival culminates a period of forty days, 'Lent', which recalls the fasting and repentance of Jesus in the wilderness.

If we imagine the year as one whole day, then Easter would be the beginning... the dawning of the day in the East. It is the only movable festival celebrated in the Christian Church as it follows the first full moon after the Spring Equinox on 21st March. The word Easter comes from an Anglo-Saxon name Eostre, or the high German Ostara who was a goddess of Spring. Much of its symbolism is connected with rebirth in nature after winter.

The period preceding Easter can be a time of questioning or reassessing our situations and searching for a way forward. There is a connection with seeking and finding... something is hidden behind the veil of nature and the earth is asleep until new life springs forth to be 'alive in us'. Because the image of resurrection is apparent in the egg (new life breaks through a hard, dead-looking shell) our practical preparation for Easter begins with the decorating of eggs. Blown (hollow) eggs may be covered with tiny pieces of wet coloured tissue paper for a lovely marbled effect, or painted with acrylic paints or thick water colours. (Remove bits of paper when the eggs have dried for the former.) Beads, lace or paper patterns can be glued on for another decorative style. Finished eggs may be hung by thread or string from a branch placed in a vase of water. This creates an Easter tree.

The Easter 'bunny' or 'hare' is a favourite picture for younger children at this festival. It is this figure who leaves baskets of flowers and chocolate eggs in some households, or hides eggs for garden hunts in others. Adults enable him to come and it helps if they know his mythical background; the hare lives alone and is a herbivore who does not harm other animals.

Stories are told of his ability to sacrifice himself when a fellow hare is being chased by a dog or fox.

In our home we make an Easter garden in advance of the festive day. It can be in the recess of the fireplace or on a large plate or tray. Starry moss or soft cloth of green create the base — the Easter tree is placed here along with a white candle, a special crystal or stone, or whatever small treasures the children add. Early primroses or violets are brought in when possible. Finally, on Easter morning itself the breakfast table is set with special care. It is lit with a special candle, the Easter bread and biscuits are added together with spring flowers.

And here then are the three components to the celebration of Easter: *food* to nurture the physical body; *plants* to feed the soul; and *the candle* to heighten the spirit.

Jane Welch.

Festival bread

'Zopf' traditional Swiss-Sunday-Breakfast bread.
Large size, plenty for 8 – 9 people.

1kg plain white flour
3 teaspoons salt
6 level teaspoons dried yeast
1 teaspoon white sugar
1pt milk
2 eggs, beaten
80 – 100g butter

Place butter and milk in a pan and heat until lukewarm. Put yeast and sugar in a bowl, add a little of the *luke*warm milk and leave until frothy.

Put flour and salt into a bowl and make a well in the centre. Pour in the yeast mixture and the rest of the milk and nearly all the egg (keep a bit of egg for painting bread just before baking). Mix to a soft dough and knead well. Let it rise until it is about double in size. Knead again and shape into the shape you want (I always plait it with four strands). Paint with egg and bake in a preheated oven at 375°F for about 45 minutes.

THE GATEWAY OF SPRING

Jehanne Mehta

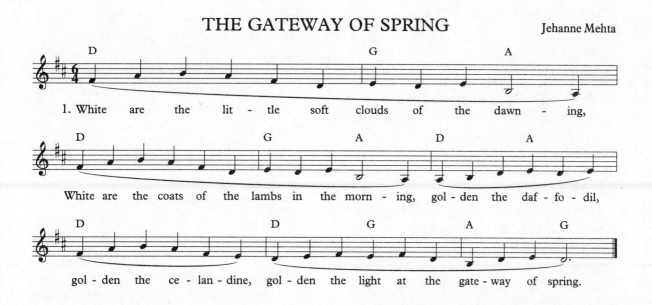

1. White are the lit - tle soft clouds of the dawn - ing,
White are the coats of the lambs in the morn - ing, gol - den the daf - fo - dil,
gol - den the ce - lan - dine, gol - den the light at the gate - way of spring.

2. Blue are the shy little violets hiding,
   Blue the great sky where the skylarks go gliding,
   Come, we will sing now, all in a ring now,
   Joyful our song as we welcome the spring.

3. Warm are the nests of the little birds calling,
   Soon to take wing on the bright air of morning,
   Easter bells chiming, Easter sun rising,
   Blessing the earth at the coming of spring.

DONA NOBIS PACEM

1. Do-na no-bis pa-cem, pacem. Do-na no-bis pa-cem.
2. Dona no-bis pacem. Dona nobis pa-cem.
3. Dona no-bis pacem. Dona nobis pa-cem.

English translation: *Give us peace.*

Thoughts from Ireland

Easter eve in candle light.

An ancient ritual welcomed Spring with great bonfires, feasting and dancing. The first fire was lit by the King himself. So it was in Ireland when young Saint Patrick came sailing up the River Boyne to the Hill of Slane. "This is where we'll celebrate Easter's Eve in a blaze of glory," said Patrick to his companions.

Away in the palace of Tara, King Laoghaire saw Patrick's bonfire shooting flames into the newly darkened sky, and he raged. The people believed that if the fire wasn't doused, then he who had lit it would reign over the land. "I'll flay him alive, the one who dared light his fire before mine!" thundered Laoghaire. "I'll peel off his skin!"

Patrick kept his skin. He told Laoghaire of the first Easter and the Irish King became a Christian, as did many of the people of Tara.

As time passed, the great bonfires slowly gave way to huge Paschal candles. As dusk deepened on Holy Saturday not a light flickered. Fires were put out. All was dark. People gathered in churches to see the great Paschal candle lit, and from it, they set ablaze their own small candles or tapers. Shielding tiny flames with cupped hands they hurried home to re-kindle their fires and lamps.

In some churches smaller Paschal candles were lit from the great one then placed where children could light their own. Spanish children however, blew out the first flame, keeping the second one flaring as they carried it in a procession of singing children marching round the walls of their church.

Jean Chapman.

Scottish texts

Joseph's tomb.

Oan that same night, wan o Jesus' supporters, a well heeled man fae Arimathea cawd Joseph, went tae Pilate an asked for the body o Jesus.

Pilate ordered the body tae be gien ower, an Joseph wrapped it up in a clean linen cloth an pit it in his ain new tomb.

Then a huge stane wis rolled ower tae stop up the door o the tomb.

The resurrection.

Early oan the Sunday mornin, Mary Magdalene an Mary the mither o James, went tae the grave takin sweet smellin ointments tae pit oan the body.

But when they got close up tae the tomb, the first thing they saw wis that the huge stane had been moved oot the wey. They went in, kinna feart-like.

All o a sudden two men wir staunin in front o them. The weemen wir terrified an cudny even look up.

The men said, "Tell us, why are ye searchin amang the graves for someone who's alive? He's no here! He's come back tae life again! D'ye no even remember whit he himsel telt ye when he wis with ye in Galilee — that the Christ must be haunded ower tae evil men, nailed tae the cross, and be raised tae life again oan the third day?"

Then, sure, they remembered whit Jesus had telt them. So they belted back in joy tae Jerusalem an telt the eleven disciples an aw the ithers, "He's alive! Jesus is alive!"

From *The Glasgow Gospel*, Jamie Stuart.

The prince of butterflies

Dame Nature, who can be everywhere at once, can see everything at once. She knows all the secrets of the plants and the pebbles and of the poor, wee creatures that make up the earth. Sometimes she makes her appearance in a single place, the better to advise and forewarn those who seek her wisdom.

Once upon a time she took up her abode in a great hollow tree, putting on a cloak as yellow as an autumn leaf and a bonnet as green as new grass. Then she sat by her door singing a song for all to hear.

"Ah! Oh!
Wonder and woe!
The sights that I see!
The things that I know!"

Among the many who heard her singing, and who stopped to listen, was an humble insect named Twig.

Twig was a caterpillar who lived in constant fear of being eaten by the hungry birds that lived in the trees. As he listened to her song, he wondered if such a wise old dame could tell him what was to become of him.

"Good-day, Granny," said Twig when the song was over.

"Good-day, good-day!" said Dame Nature kindly. "What can I do for you, my child?"

"I am only a caterpillar," Twig said meekly, "but I would like to be happy. As it is, I am usually in such danger of being swallowed by a hungry bird that I can never enjoy myself."

"Even when there are no birds around, I am not very happy. My poor head is full of strange ideas. It seems I shall never be happy unless I can fly. Of course I have no wings and I don't know what is to become of me."

"And if you wish to fly, you shall," said Dame Nature with a gleam in her eye. "Be patient and never fear, for the time will come when you will fly through the air on golden wings, as high as any bird."

"How can that be possible?" whispered Twig, trembling with excitement. "How can it be?"

"Nevertheless it is true," said she, nodding wisely, "but before you are ready to fly, you must learn an important secret. Once you have learned that secret, you will fall sound asleep with many a dream to keep you happy. When you awake, you will look at yourself to see that I was right."

"Can it be true? Can it be true?" cried Twig. "To think that I shall fly! How beautiful it will be! Who am I, to have golden wings?"

As he went on his way, he wept for joy.

In a few days' time he was quite used to the idea and he spoke of it to all of his friends.

"It may interest you to know that soon I shall be able to fly," he said to them mysteriously.

"Indeed!" said the ant. "In that case I must learn how to swim."

"One needs wings before he can fly, my poor Twig," said the beetle.

"That will be fine," said the spider, "but take care not to fly into my web."

Their answers made Twig wish that he had not said anything. How could he expect them to believe him? When the time came, they could see for themselves and until then he would keep away from them.

So he went off by himself and tried to be patient, wondering what secret he would learn; but there was no one to tell him any secrets. Whenever he went to sleep, he dreamed that all the birds in the world were flapping around him, and he would wake up in a great fright only to see that he was as far from flying as ever.

"The old dame must have been wrong," he said mournfully. "I expect I shall spend the rest of my life crawling around without any wings, only to be swallowed by a hateful bird in the end."

As he wandered through the grass, he came face to face with his friend, the ant, who made fun of him, saying, "Still crawling about I see!"

Twig did not answer. When the ant had gone, he wept in despair and, as there was no one to comfort him, he hurried back to find Dame Nature to see what she would say.

There she sat by the door of her hollow tree, in her yellow cloak and green bonnet, singing:

"Come what may,
Go what may,
Come and go what may,
I see the sights
And know the things
That happen far away!"

When she had finished her song, she spoke to Twig. "Oh-ho," she said, "so you are back again and you are feeling sad for no reason at all. That is a pity."

"I have good reason to be sad," grumbled Twig.

"All you said about secrets and dreams and golden wings hasn't helped me out of my troubles. No one has told me any secrets, and each time I go to sleep I have bad dreams that frighten me to death. So, in spite of what you said, I don't know what will become of me."

"You are an impatient creature," said the wise old dame in a stern voice. "It won't help you to grumble and fuss. Go home and keep your patience. When you are ready to fly, you will."

"If I were only sure!" wailed the caterpillar as he went home again. "I think it is harder to wait for things to happen than never to have them happen at all."

Once he had made up his mind to be patient, time passed quite pleasantly. He became so used to waiting that he was almost happy.

And then, one morning, as he looked around him, everything seemed changed. Each blade of grass was swaying in the breeze. The flowers were very gay, nodding their heads and whispering among themselves; and there were no bird voices in the rustling trees overhead.

"What a lovely world this is!" said Twig very softly. "I may be a caterpillar of no importance but in by heart I am flying higher than any bird and that is all that matters."

As he finished speaking, he remembered that Dame Nature had said, "Before you fly, you must learn an important secret." Now he was sure he knew the secret.

Suddenly he felt very sleepy, so he wrapped himself snugly in a leaf and went right to sleep. In his dreams he chased the wind over the tops of the tallest trees and floated to earth in showers of sunbeams, only to rise with the wind again. He never knew how long he slept. His dreams were so sweet that even the cold snows of winter did not disturb him.

When, at last, he awoke to crawl out of his leaf-blanket, he knew that he was still himself and yet he felt like someone else. He had fewer legs and they felt very weak. As he rested in the warm, spring sunshine, they grew stronger and he stood up. Then he discovered that he was wearing a close-fitting cloak. As it slowly spread out around him, he trembled with joy.

"How beautiful they are, how beautiful!" he whispered, fluttering his wings slowly up and down while the sunbeams sprinkled them with gold. Each moment they grew stronger until finally they lifted him away from the ground, high into the air.

He flew about very carefully so as to get used to them and then went straight to the hollow tree in search of his well-remembered friend, Dame Nature. And there she was, on her doorstep, singing one of her songs:

"Yesterday was,
Tomorrow will be,
But they're one and the same to me.
The dreams of Kings
And of smaller things
Are plain for me to see."

"Good-day, Granny," he said when she had finished her song.

"Good-day, good-day," she answered, "and what can I do for you, my child?"

"I have come to show you my wings," he said, fluttering them gracefully before her. "They are such beautiful wings but a bit hard to manage as yet."

"So I see," said Dame Nature, with a twinkle in her eye, "and poor Twig, with all his troubles, is now the Prince of Butterflies!"

Dorothy Harrer.

Colouring hard-boiled eggs

There are many commercial egg dyes and food colourings available for making hard-boiled eggs bright and beautiful for Easter Day. If you would like to try for more natural and subtle forms of dying, experiment with the following:

Orange peel for light yellow;
Pear peelings for yellow-green;
Onion skins for deep orange-brown;
Red cabbage for blue;
Cranberries for purple-red;
Beetroot for pink.

Gather as much of your chosen colour source ingredient as possible and bring to a boil in a non-aluminium saucepan. (The larger quantity of peel, onion skin, berry, etc, will give you more defined colour.) Add eggs and reduce to a gentle boil. Add a teaspoon or two of vinegar and make sure your dye batch covers the eggs completely. Fifteen minutes is a reasonable boiling time.

When eggs are cool, rub with a bit of margarine or vegetable oil (on a bit of cloth) to bring to a glossy shine.

Baisakhi festival

Baisakhi day is celebrated on 13th April by both Sikhs and Hindus as the first day of the New Year. In the Punjab it also marks the end of the Spring wheat harvest.

Baisakhi day is also celebrated by Sikhs as the day that Guru Gobind Singh founded the Khalsa movement in 1699. The festival lasts for three days, two of which are spent reading the Guru Granth Sahib in the Gurdwara. Five men take it in turns to read the sacred text for two hours at a time. When the reading is complete, new members of the Khalsa are admitted into the fellowship of the Khalsa. They drink Amrit and receive the 5 'K's.

In some cities members of the Khalsa, dressed in saffron yellow, carry ceremonial swords in a procession through the streets from the Gurdwara.

The whole congregation gathers together at the end of the festival for hymns and prayers. The fruit and karah parshad (sugar, water, ghee, semolina) is shared out among the congregation before everyone eats together in the langar (free kitchen). The langar is open after every act of worship and not just at Baisakhi. Sikhs volunteer to prepare and serve the food to each other in the langar. The meal often consists of pakora dhal and vegetable curries which are eaten with pieces of chappati, a bready pancake. Anyone is welcome to share the food in the langar whatever their colour, religion, social circumstances or nationality. Sikhs believe that everyone is equal and they must share what they have with others as a practical expression of God's teaching.

The founding of the Khalsa

Guru Gobind Singh was the tenth of the human Gurus. A guru is a Sikh holy teacher.

On Baisakhi day in 1699 Guru Gobind Singh called all Sikhs together to a meeting in Andanpus. The Sikh people were peace loving but they were being attacked and killed because of their religious beliefs.

Guru Gobind Singh realised that in order for the Sikhs to defeat their enemies they had to be prepared to be strong and always ready to fight for their faith.

On Baisakhi day, Guru Boblin of Singh stood before his people in full saffron yellow battle uniform wearing his long sword and his bow and arrows. He told all the Sikhs that they must unite together as one people, he drew his sword and he asked if anyone among them was prepared to die for his faith.

Everyone was frightened because they did not want to die so after a few minutes the guru repeated his question. "Is there anyone among you who is prepared to die for his faith?" There was still no response so the guru asked the same question for a third time.

One man stepped forward and as he stood before Guru Gobind Singh he said, "I will die for you, you can take my head."

Everyone else was silent as the guru led the man to a tent nearby. In the silence they heard a loud thud before Guru Gobind Singh returned to them. In his hand he carried his long sword which was covered in fresh blood. He asked again if anyone else was prepared to die for their faith. Another man stepped forward and told the guru that he could take his head because he was prepared to die for him.

The man and the guru walked to the tent and once again in the silence the crowd heard a loud thud before the guru returned to them with his long sword covered in blood.

This happened again until the people in the crowd became quite worried and some of them began to think that Guru Gobind Singh had gone mad.

After a fifth man had entered the tent with him, the guru returned to the crowd followed by all five men who were now dressed in saffron yellow uniforms like the uniform worn by the guru and carrying long swords. The Sikhs in the crowd were delighted that the guru had not killed the five men.

Guru Gobind Singh announced that the five men were the first five members of the Sikh brotherhood called the Khalsa. He explained that because these five men had been courageous enough to give up their lives for the Sikh faith they were to be known as the *Panj Pyares*, (the beloved five).

To each of these five men Guru Gobind Singh gave five things. As each of these things begin with the letter 'K' in Punjabi they are known as the 'Five Ks'.

Firstly they were given a short curved sword known as a Kirpan to show their willingness to fight in the defence of their faith and to protect the weak and helpless. Next they were given a steel bangle — the kara — to remind them that the Khalsa is joined together in unity. A command was also given to them, never to cut their hair but always to wear it long (kesh), and to keep their hair clean and tidy with a fine toothed comb called a kangha. The kangha was worn in the long hair to remind them of the tidy, well ordered lives they should lead. Finally a pair of loosely fitting shorts, the kachs, made of white cotton to give them freedom of movement when they were fighting in battles to defend their faith.

Each one of the panj pyares came from a different caste or level of sociey and there had been great prejudice between the castes. Guru Gobind Singh knew that in God's eyes all humans are equal so he initiated the panj pyares into the holy order of the Khalsa. He asked them to drink amrit from the same bowl to demonstrate that they were equal. Amrit is sugar and water in a steel bowl which had been stirred by a double edged sword called Khanda.

On that Baisakhi day in 1699 the guru told all Sikhs to take the name Singh (lion) if they were men and Kaur (princess) if they were women.

To this day all Sikhs are called Singh or Kaur. However, because it is more usual in western culture for families to share the same name, the wife will take Singh as her surname. Sometimes the wife and children will take the husband's family name but will include Singh or Kaur within that name, for example: Narinder Kaur Kapoor.

The five Ks of Sikhism

A Kirpan is worn to show a willingness to fight for their faith.

The Kara, a steel bangle, is worn to remember that the khalsa is joined in unity.

The hair is always worn long (Kesh) and never cut.

The hair is kept clean and tidy with a Kangha.

The Kachs are worn to give freedom of movement when fighting to defend the faith.

A story for Baisakhi

In the rich Indian farming state of the Punjab, harvest comes, not in August or September, as in Europe, but in April. Just before the summer starts to get so hot that the earth cracks and the leaves hang limp on the trees, they gather in the wheat and Sikhs joyfully prepare to celebrate Baisakhi, which is their name for April.

Baisakhi marks the beginning of the Sikh new year. It celebrates the birth of the Khalsa, the Brotherhood of the Pure Ones. It is the time when new members, both men and women, can be initiated into the Brotherhood.

Behind the serious and deeply religious quality of the ceremony, Sikhs will all know the enjoyable fable which they tell again and again to their children. It is the story of a donkey, which their revered saint, Guru Gobind Singh told his followers at Baisakhi, to illustrate the moral that you are what you wear:

There was once a poor donkey, whose whole life had been one of hardship. Day after day, his master burdened him with such loads, that his knobbly, weak legs could hardly totter from one place to another.

One day, as he was staggering along, the donkey bumped into a tree in which a hunter had hung out animal skins to dry. The bump shook the branches, and down fell the skin of a lion and covered the mangy creature.

Unknowingly, the donkey shuffled home, but to his surprise, as he entered the yard, his master took one look at him and fled. The other animals in the yard, who normally looked down on him, they too, turned and ran away. They didn't come back, even when he began to eat their food. The donkey wandered about the yard, bewildered. Why, even when he began to munch in the vegetable patch, his master's wife didn't rush out to beat him with a stick as she usually did.

The gate was still open, and as there was no one to stop him, the donkey wandered out into the street. Why did the melon stall holder not wallop him, when he stopped to munch some juicy melons? Why did it seem that, wherever he went, people ran away, and watched him from a safe distance? Why did even the tiger run away from him when he went to the waterhole to drink?

When night fell, the donkey wanted to go home, but when he returned to his master's house, the gate was locked and barred so, fearfully, he went back to the jungle.

For some months, the donkey lived all alone. No animal or human being would come near him. It made him sad. He longed for company, even for his master who beat him. One day, he saw his master passing by and the donkey trotted after him braying, "Hee haw! Hee haw!" but his master looked astonished and backed away. "What is this? A lion that brays like a donkey?" he cried, and would have fled once more, except, at that moment, the skin on the donkey's back got caught on a low branch. It whisked the lion's guise off his back, and revealed him for what he was.

"Why you cheating animal!" exclaimed the master, and picking up a stick, ran up to the donkey and beat him without mercy all the way home.

The poor donkey never did understand what had happened — not to his dying day.

Recipes for Baisakhi

Karah Parshad:

150g granulated sugar
1 litre water
75g raisins
1 tablespoon chopped almonds
½ teaspoon cardomom seeds
125g ghee (or butter)
125g semolina

Dissolve the sugar in the water. Add the raisins, chopped almonds and cardomom seeds. Heat the ghee (clarified butter) or butter in a heavy bottomed saucepan and fry the semolina gently until it begins to turn golden brown. Add the sweetened, flavoured water to the semolina, stirring all the time. Heat gently until the semolina has softened and the liquid is absorbed.

Serve the karah parshad while it is still warm.

Chappati:

250g wholemeal flour
1 teaspoon salt
200ml water

Put the flour and salt into a bowl. Make a well in the centre of the flour and gradually pour in the water mixing the ingredients into a soft dough. Knead the dough well for several minutes. The children will enjoy this part. Cover the dough in the bowl with a cloth and leave for 20 minutes. Knead the dough again then divide into 12 pieces. Roll each piece of dough, on a well floured board, until it resembles a thin pancake.

Heat a lightly oiled heavy frying pan over a medium heat. Add the first chappati and cook for about 1 minute until it bubbles. Turn and cook the other side until the edges of the chappati begin to turn golden brown. Keep hot until all twelve are cooked. Serve warm with savoury dishes.

Make a flag and garland

Make a saffron yellow flag in either paper or fabric and paint or draw on it a black Khanda, the Sikh symbol.

Garlands are worn round the neck for special occasions or can be hung as a decoration.

Use sequins, tinsel, gold and silver pens and shiny paper to make your garland as colourful as possible.

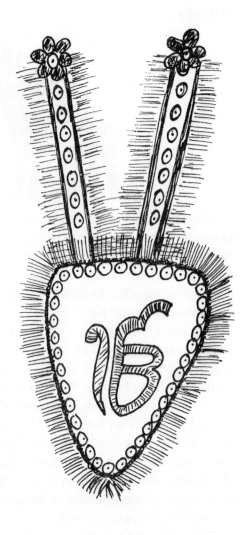

The symbol of the Khanda can be seen outside a Gudwara. The Khanda consists of three symbols in one. The Khanda itself is a double edged sword which symbolises truth. The circle or chakkar symbolises the oneness of God. The two kirpans symbolise both spiritual and earthly strength.

Make a glittering garland.

The characters of the symbol are the first words — Ik Onkar — of the Sikh prayer called the Mool Mantra.

The words can be translated as "There is only one God."

9. WESAK

May full moon

This is a special night commemorating the birth, enlightenment and death of the Buddha — all of which took place some 2,500 years ago.

In Thailand people clean their homes and hang up garlands of flowers, streamers and flags. Buddha statues are washed and cleaned until they shine.

As a young boy, the Buddha went by his given name "Siddhartha". He enjoyed sport, nature, and his schooling. It is said that he had a particular love for all living creatures — great or small.

One day he was out walking in the forest with his cousin Devadatta. Devadatta was a keen hunter and carried a bow and arrows. When a swan flew overhead he took aim and shot it. As the bird fell both boys ran to find it, with Siddhartha arriving first. The swan was still alive although the arrow had pierced its wing. Gently Siddhartha pulled the arrow out. He pressed leaves on the wound to stop the bleeding and spoke gently to the frightened swan.

Devadatta arrived on the scene. He insisted that the bird was his, for he had shot it! The cousins argued, for Siddhartha said that a hunter could only claim an animal if he killed it. They finally decided to take their argument to the wise men of the palace.

The wise men listened carefully to the two boys. Then they declared that a life must belong to him who tries to save it. It cannot be claimed by someone who tries to destroy it. Siddhartha had the right to care for the wounded swan. So he took it, and nursed it, and when it had recovered, the swan flew away.

Already Siddhartha had shown his understanding of what would be one of his greatest lessons for the world — that of compassion.

If you visit Buddhist temples in south-east Asia, you may still find a custom of setting song birds free from little bamboo or wicker cages at the temple entrance.

Make a lotus flower

Symbol of purity and truth.

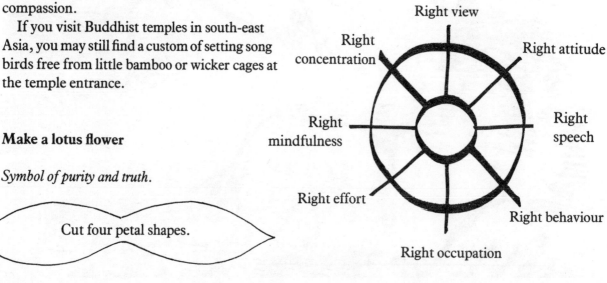

Cut four petal shapes.

Place one shape on top of the other, spacing them evenly as in a circle.

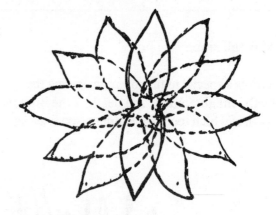

Glue down individually or staple through all four shapes at the centre.

Gently curl petals inwards with the blade of some scissors or roll the petal from the tip around a pencil.

Lotus flowers are usually pink. Either cut the shapes from pink paper or shade the edges of the petals with pink crayon or felt pen.

The eight-fold path to enlightenment

Right view

Right attitude

Right speech

Right behaviour

Right occupation

Right effort

Right mindfulness

Right concentration

A procession of elephants

Cut out several elephant shapes in thin card.

Decorate them with sequins, scraps of shiny fabric or braid.

Colour some of the elephants in bright colours with felt tipped pens.

The life of the Buddha

More than 2,500 years ago in the foothills of the beautiful Himalayan mountains of India, a baby boy was born in a place we now call Nepal. The boy's father who was a king was delighted with his son and he arranged a special celebration when the baby was named. Among the guests he invited some wise men who could look into the future to say what was in store for the baby. The baby was named Siddhartha.

Gautama and all the wise men, apart from one, agreed that Prince Siddhartha would become a great king. The other wise man said that once Prince Siddhartha saw any suffering in the world he would leave home and become a great teacher. He would devote his life to helping others.

The words of this last wise man worried the king who wanted his son to become king after him and to rule his kingdom. So the king decided that he would surround Prince Siddhartha with beautiful palaces, fine clothing, good food and fit and healthy young people so that suffering would never enter his world.

Prince Siddhartha grew up and married a lovely young bride called Yasodhara and soon they had a son of their own.

One day Prince Siddhartha asked his friend Chanha to take him for a drive in his chariot, outside the palace grounds. During the drive the prince demanded that Chanha should stop the chariot. He had seen a very old man for the first time and Chanha had to explain to him about old age. Prince Siddhartha demanded that the chariot was stopped again when he saw a very sick man with a diseased body and again Chanha had to explain that sometimes people become very ill and suffer great pain. A little further down, the road Prince Siddhartha heard people crying pitifully because someone they loved had died. The body was being carried to the funeral. He was very shocked to hear from Chanha that everyone must die.

Prince Siddartha was troubled by the things

After that Siddhartha began to eat a little food regularly to build up his strength and stopped treating his body harshly. The five holy men were appalled at his new behaviour and left him. He sat alone under a bodhi tree to think very deeply about truth and suffering.

When he finally understood what truth is he was said to have received light, to become enlightened. After this he became known as Buddha. This means 'the enlightened one,' the one who understands.

He spent the next forty-five years preaching to all sorts of people rich and poor, young and old, until he died at the age of eighty. Many people try to follow the way of life and the teaching of Buddha so that they too may receive the light.

he had seen on his journey. For the first time in his life he knew that there was great suffering in the world and that not everyone led carefree lives like him. When they were almost back at the palace Prince Siddhartha saw a wandering holy man with a shaved head wearing a rough brown robe. He asked Chanha what the man was doing. Chanha explained that the holy man lived on his own, spending all his time thinking about the serious side of life.

Siddhartha spent several days thinking about the four disturbing sights he had encountered on his journey. He decided that he must leave his home, his family and his riches to become a holy man himself to see if he could find a way to end all pain and suffering.

He gave up fine robes and jewellery for the rough brown robe of a holy man.

Siddhartha wandered around until he found five very holy men who told him that he had to treat his body harshly if he was to understand the meaning of suffering. So he exposed himself to the hot sun and the cold nights, he refused to eat until he became very, very ill and had almost killed himself, before he realized that he was not approaching the question the right way.

'Wesak' or Buddha Day

Wesak (Visakha) is the most important festival in the Buddhist calendar. Many Buddhists celebrate the birth, enlightenment and death of Gautama Buddha on this day because all these great events in the Buddha's life occurred on the same day but in different years. The festival is celebrated in May/June of the Western calendar. There are no special foods attached to this festival as it is not a feast day.

In Britain, temples (Vihara) and shrines in the home are decorated with lanterns, candles, flowers and garlands. Wesak cards are sent from one Buddhist to another illustrated with pictures of the Bodhi tree, events in the life of Buddha or of the lotus flower which is a symbol of purity and truth.

Sacred scriptures are read by monks in the Vihara and it is a custom for Buddhists visiting the Vihara to give the monks gifts (alms) at Wesak. In Thailand, where there are many Buddhists, beautiful decorated elephants lead a procession through the streets.

Buddhists do not worship the Buddha as god but they try to follow the teachings and way of life of the Buddha. One of his most important teachings was the need for everyone to follow the Noble Eightfold path which symbolically is represented by the eight spokes in the Buddhist Wheel of Life.

10. FLOWER FESTIVALS

Flower festivals

From the daffodils in St David's, cherry blossom in Kyoto, brilliant garlands in Bangalore, to Mayday baskets of early blooms in Kansas City, or tulip fields in Holland, the flower festival finds different forms in different places. Celebrate spring in home or classroom by planting and decorating! Choose hardy annuals which will thrive in simple pot surroundings — nasturtiums, marigolds, pansies, etc. If there are no fresh flowers to bring into the room, enjoy creating 'other' flowers!

How to make the flowers

Tissue paper
Scissors
Needle and thread
Small beads

1. Cut squares of coloured tissue.

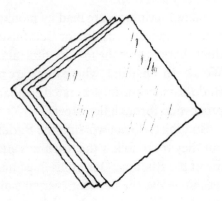

2. Fold several layers into a smaller square.

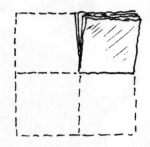

3. Cut off the corners to make petal shapes.

4. Open out the tissue.

5. With a needle and thread, secure the layers together and arrange them into flowers.

You can also cut out leaf-shapes to attach to the flowers.

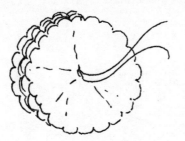

Flower chains:

Try making chains of flowers and leaves, threading them together with a needle and thread.

Experiment with different colours, shapes and sizes. Small beads can also be used to separate leaves and flowers.

Window boxes

A large piece of strong card
Coloured tissue paper
Stanley knife or scissors
Glue
Paints

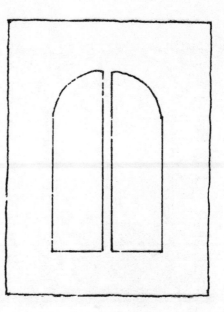

1. Cut out the shape of the window.

2. Paint the window frame and the stone or brick wall.

3. Use the left-over card for a window box; colour it and glue it in place.

4. Glue a piece of tissue onto the back of the window.
5. For a stained glass window effect, stick on torn pieces of tissue and cut out shapes, with different colours.

6. Now fill the window box with flowers.

BLOSSOM SONG

Japanese traditional

Sa - ku - ra! sa - ku - ra! Ya - yo - i no so - ra - wa,

Mi - wa - ta - su ka - ghi - ri; Ka - su - mi ka? ku - mo_ ka? Ni - o - i zo

i - zu - ru; I - za - ya! i - za - ya! Mi - ni yu - ka - n.

Cherry trees! Cherry trees!
Bloom so bright,
In April breeze;
Like a mist or floating cloud,
Fragrance fills the air around,
Shadows flit along the ground.
Come o come! Come o come!
Come, see cherry trees!

III
SUMMER

1. SUMMER SUN

Why the sun shines when the cock crows

Traditional tale, Hanai origins, southern China.

Once upon a time, the earth was surrounded by many suns. To the east shone one sun, another in the west; there was one in the north and one in the south. And in between these were five smaller suns! There was also the sun we know today in our sky.

As you can well imagine, the earth was scorched. No grass could grow, and people were too hot and tired to work or sleep. So one day the wise elders of the world met to think what to do. They decided to ask the giant Oppopolo to shoot down the suns so that the poor earth could feel coolness again.

Oppopolo lived on top of the highest mountain and was as tall as ten ordinary men. His body was strong and his eyes flashed with bravery. Two citizens climbed the mountain with the elders' request, and the giant agreed to help.

So it was that the very next day when the first sun rose over the horizon, he took his mighty bow and shot it down. The people cheered with joy. Another speedy arrow brought down the second sun, then the third, fourth, fifth and more. At first the people danced with glee. But by the time the ninth sun fell, they were rather chilly and worried. As the tenth sun had watched everything, he hid behind the mountain. The earth was dark as night and cold as winter ice.

"Stop, Oppopolo, stop!" cried the people. They begged for the remaining sun to return but he refused to leave his hiding place of safety!

It was decided that someone must plead with the sun, but as it might now fear a human, a bird would be sent instead. First the nightingale went as messenger, singing sweetly. The sun refused to listen. Then the thrush tried, and the lark, and the blackbird. But it was no use. At last the cockerel was asked if he would try. "All right," he replied, "But I can't sing. All I can do is crow."

The cockerel lifted his neck and crowed loudly. When he did this the sun didn't recognise the noise, and as it came again the sun peeped out, curiously. As his light appeared from behind the mountain the birds, animals and people all shouted and sang with joy! The sun was pleased, and felt bold enough to show himself in full. So, to this day the sun hides at night until the cock's crow tells him it is safe again to come out!

Eagle chases chickens

A game from old Hong Kong for six to eighteen players.

To begin the game one child is 'Eagle' and one is 'Mother Hen'. The rest become 'baby chickens'.

Mother Hen leads the chickens to form a single line facing one direction. Each child puts his arms around the waist of the child in front of him or her.

To start, Eagle must stand facing Mother Hen from a distance of four or five feet. At the signal to play Eagle must run towards the chicken at the end of the line, attempting to tag him. The Mother Hen and chickens try to prevent this by swinging the line to and fro — while keeping the line intact!

If the chicken is tagged by Eagle, he becomes the next Eagle. The earlier eagle goes to the head of the children, becoming Mother Hen. Then the game begins again.

Paul Wong.

2. MIDSUMMER

Celebration of Summer Solstice — the longest day of the year.

On a midsummer eve

I idly cut a parsley stalk
And blew therein towards the moon;
I had not thought what ghosts would walk
With shivering footsteps to my tune.

I went, and knelt, and scooped my hand
As if to drink, into the brook,

And a faint figure seemed to stand
Above me, with the bygone look.

I lipped rough rhymes of chance, not choice,
I thought not what my words might be;
There came into my ear a voice
That turned a tenderer verse for me.

Thomas Hardy.

SUN FIRE

Jehanne Mehta

Two part round and dance for midsummer

To light the sun fire in this __ land we car - ry a torch, we
kindle the sun warmth in all __ hearts we of - fer our song, we

car - ry a brand. To of - fer our dance. When swir - ling flames with

red tongues fly and grey smoke bil-lows to the __ sky, Then shall the dark-ness

burn __ a - way __ In the sing - ing sun __ fire of Mid-sum-mer's Day. __ To...

dal segno 𝄋

Sun fire circle dance

Holding hands and facing centre ('fire') throughout:

1. Starting on right foot, take two slow steps towards the centre, raising arms high.
2. Two steps back, lowering arms.
3. Raising arms to shoulder height, step to the right with right foot and close with left foot ('torches').
4. Step to the left with left foot and close with right, arms still holding 'torches'.
5. Same as (1).
6. Same as (2).
7. Step to the right and point left foot towards centre and bow (offering).
8. Step to the left and point right foot towards centre and bow.

9. Sixteen small running steps round to the right, starting on right foot, swinging arms in and out (flames).
10. Four small running steps into centre, raising arms high.
11. Four small running steps back, lowering arms.
12. As (10).
13. As (11).

An alternative version of (9) is the Grapevine step: Going to the right, step on the right foot, step behind with left foot. Step on right again and step in front with left foot. Repeat three times more.

Summer magic

The story of Urashimo Taro, the young fisherman.

Long, long ago in the little fishing village of Mitzu-no-re, on the shores of Japan, there lived a young fisherman named Urashimo Taro. His father had been a fisherman before him, and his grandfather before that, and all the skills of the sea and of fishing had been handed on to Urashimo. Far and wide it was known that Urashimo often caught more fish in a day than others could in a week.

But he was well known for his kind heart even more than for being a clever fisherman. In his whole life he had never hurt anything, either great or small. As a small boy his friends would laugh at him because he would not join them in teasing animals. He, in turn, tried to tell them that this was cruel sport.

One soft summer twilight he was on his way home after a day's fishing when he came upon an excited group of children. They were all screaming gleefully and jumping this way and that. Out of curiosity he went to have a look, only to discover that they were tormenting a tortoise, pulling it this way and that, hitting it on its shell with a stick, and even throwing pebbles at it. "Look here!" cried Urashimo, "you are treating that tortoise so badly it could die soon!"

The children took no notice but went on teasing it as before. One of the older boys even answered, "Who cares whether it lives or not", and began hitting it even harder.

Urashimo tried again. "Stop!" he said, taking a string of coins from his pocket. "Let me buy the tortoise from you. You can do much more with this money than you can with a simple tortoise. How about it?"

Now the children were not bad children really; they were carried away in the moment but these words drew their attention. They came to gaze at the coins and listen to Urashimo. He talked to them gently with a kind smile, and as they listened they began to agree and to 'be of his spirit,' as they say in Japan. Indeed, at last they handed him the tortoise and walked away with their money. And Urashimo hugged the frightened creature to him and stroked its back, saying, "There, there, poor thing. Tortoises never hurt anybody, and we have stopped them hurting you! They say that a stork lives for a thousand years, but a tortoise for ten thousand years! Think of the time for peace and a good life ahead of you. Now I will take you back to your home, the sea. Mind you don't let yourself be caught by humans again!"

He walked down the shore and out on the rocks. Then, after carefully putting the tortoise into the water so that it could swim away, he returned home in the sunset.

The next day the young fisherman went out as usual in his boat. It was a fine morning with blue sea and sky. Urashimo drifted further and further out on the waters, casting in his line and thinking dreamily what it must be like to live for one thousand years or more, like a stork or tortoise. The sun rose, warming his back, and suddenly his own name was called! "Urashimo, Urashimo!" As clear as a bell and soft as the summer wind, his name floated over the sea.

He stood up and looked in every direction, thinking another boat must be close by — but there was no sign of anything but water, water and sky line. He was too far from the shore to see land or people, and not a boat was in sight. "Urashimo!" came the voice again, and in amazement he saw his friend the tortoise swimming by the side of his boat.

"Mr Tortoise," Urashimo cried, "is it you who calls my name so clearly?"

The tortoise nodded its head several times.

"Yesterday you saved my life and I have come to offer my thanks."

"Indeed," said Urashimo, "that is very kind of you. Come up into my boat and sun yourself."

The tortoise accepted this invitation and climbed up slowly. After a bit of polite chatter the tortoise asked, "Have you ever seen Rin Gin, the palace of the dragon king of the sea, Urashimo?"

The fisherman shook his head. He had heard many tales of the dragon king's kingdom under the sea. There were legends and stories from ancient times, but no one knew of the truth in them. "It must be very far away," he said doubtfully, "if it exists at all."

The tortoise spoke very solemnly, "it is one of the most wonderful sights in the whole world. It is far, far away, at the bottom of the deepest sea. But if I take you, we will soon be there. Sit on my back and you will have a journey you will never forget." As he spoke, the tortoise grew so large that Urashimo saw this was indeed possible. Full of the wonder of it all he climbed onto the strong shell and held on tight.

Down through the water dived the tortoise with the fisherman on his back. Through depths of colour and schools of small fish they flew; yet the young man never lost his breath, never felt cold or even wet! The water was a new world for him, and long they rode together. At last, far away in the distance a magnificent gate could be seen and behind it the sloping roofs of a coral palace. "That is the great gate of the Rin Gin palace and behind it the palace, itself!" said the tortoise.

The gatekeeper, who was a fish, greeted them as they came closer, and led the way for them. The red bream, the flounder, the sole and the cuttlefish all came and bowed to greet the stranger. "This is Urashimo Taro. I have the honour to bring him as guest to this kingdom"

announced the tortoise.

Urashimo, being a poor fisherman, did not know how to behave in a palace, but followed the courtly fish through doorways and gilded halls until they reached the inner palace. A beautiful princess with her helping maidens came to greet him. She was more beautiful than any human being, and robed in waves of red and green garments, with golden threads glimmering through her gown. Her lovely black hair streamed over her shoulders and her voice was like music. Urashimo did not even think to bow. She took him by the hand and led him to a seat of honour. The fish guides stood by him, but the tortoise was nowhere to be seen.

The princess spoke. "Urashimo Taro, it is a high pleasure to welcome you to my father's kingdom. Yesterday you set free a sea creature, and I have sent for you to thank you. For yesterday I had taken the form of a tortoise, and you saved my life. We may rejoice here, and if you like you may live in this land of eternal youth, where summer never dies, where sorrow never comes. If you like, I will be your bride, and you will live in splendour here."

Urashimo was filled with joy, and feeling as though in a dream, he thanked the princess and said he would love to stay. Gold and silver fish appeared with fine wedding clothes, with a feast of food and magical music. In a palace built of coral and decorated with pearls, Urashimo married the sea king's daughter. In the days that followed, he came to know his surroundings.

There was a garden more wonderful than any garden. Here you could see the scenery of four different seasons all at once. To the east were the plum and cherry blossom, singing nightingales and butterflies in flight. To the south, the trees had the full green of summer and crickets chirped loud and contentedly. To the west were red autumn maple leaves and golden chrysanthemums. And to the north gleamed silver white snow and a pond thick with ice. So great was the awe and so many the discoveries that the young man forgot everything — the village and home he had left behind, his parents and his own country. Then gradually his memory came back, and he thought of his dear old father and mother who must be worrying about him. He began to prepare to go home to them, and went to tell the princess. "Otohime Sama," he said (for that was her name) I have been happy with you in this fine land and you have been good and kind to me. But I must go back to visit my old parents. I must say good-bye."

The beautiful princess began to weep. When she saw that she could not change his mind, she brought out a shining black lacquer box tied with red silk cord. "If you go," she said, "you must take this with you. It is the Box of the Jewel Hand and contains something very precious. Please never, never open it, or something dreadful will happen. Never open it. Just carry it as a token of my love." And Urashimo promised never to open it.

He bade good-bye to Otohime Sama and left on the back of a great tortoise which carried him over the sea to Japan. At last they came to the shoreline and bay which he knew so well, and the tortoise gently left him on the land there. Urashimo knew the hills which faced him, he knew the rocks near the waves. But a strange fear took hold him, for the faces and clothing of the fishermen ahead were totally different to the friends he remembered. He walked quickly to his old village, which also seemed strange, and found his home, calling "Father, I have returned! Mother, your son is home again!"

A man he did not recognize came to the door. What was this? Had his parents moved house? "Excuse me, I am Urashimo Taro. Where have my parents gone?"

The man looked bewildered. "What?" he replied, "You are Urashimo Taro? You must not make such a joke! Once such a fellow did live in our village, but that was three hundred years ago!"

Urashimo felt frightened and confused. He asked the man not to joke with him, saying he had only been gone a short while! He stomped his feet on the ground to show he was not a ghost from the past, for it was then thought that ghosts had no feet! The man in the doorway shook his head. "It is written in the village records." he insisted. "The fisherman Urashimo Taro lived three hundred years ago. That is all I know."

Urashimo felt completely lost now. It was true that everything around him seemed completely different to his memory of the place and people. The few days he had spent in the sea king's palace must not have been days, at all. It had been hundreds of human years, and in that time all that he had known had died away. He must get back to his wife and kingdom in the sea.

He walked back to the beach, carrying in his hand the box which the princess had given him.

How would he find his way back? He looked at the box, the Tamate-Bako. He had promised never to open it, but perhaps it might hold a clue for him now. "Yes," he thought, "I will open the box and look in!" Slowly he untied the red silk, knowing he had promised not to. He lifted the lid of the precious box. What did he find?

Strange to say, only a beautiful little purple cloud rose out in three soft wisps. It drifted away towards the sea. And Urashimo, who until that moment had been a strong handsome youth of twenty-four, suddenly became very, very old. His back doubled up with age, his hair turned white, and he disappeared on the beach! All time caught up with him when he opened that special box. But his story lives on — to remind us to be kind to animals, to keep our promises, and to marvel at mysteries under the sea!

Adapted from T. Ozaki, "The Story of Urashimo Taro, The Fisher Lad" in *The Golden Pathway*.

3. MIDSUMMER RECIPES

Grapefruit or orange baskets

These pretty baskets are perfect for any festive occasion.

1 large grapefruit or large orange
1 slice fresh pineapple
1 slice dessert mango
A few slices banana
3 or 4 cherries
1 tablespoon lime juice
¼ cup (50g) granulated sugar
⅛ cup (30ml) water or fruit juice

First boil the sugar and water or fruit juice together until it is slightly thickened to make a light syrup. Leave this to cool.

To make the basket, wash the orange or grapefruit and cut it almost in half from both sides, leaving about 2cm (¾″) uncut towards the centre. Leaving this central band of 2cm (¾″), cut away the top two 'quarters' downwards to the centre and remove these sections. Use a fruit knife to cut the fruit from the remaining semicircle to form a handle. Remove all the fruit from the basket and scrape out all the pith.

Finely chop the mango and pineapple into a small bowl, add slices of banana and some of the grapefruit or orange sections. Squeeze the lime juice over the fruit and then pour on the syrup.

Fill the basket with the fruit mixture and garnish it with sliced cheries. Chill before serving.

An extra special touch is made by tying a pretty ribbon to the handle of the basket before serving.

You can vary the fruit in the basket depending on what is available. For a child's party you can even fill fruit baskets with jelly of a contrasting colour.

Oranges and lemons

A game for younger children.

Two children are chosen to hold hands and form an arch, one to be Oranges, the other Lemons. The other children, forming a chain, march underneath singing the song:

"Oranges and lemons," say the bells of St
　　Clement's,
"You owe me five farthings," say the bells of St
　　Martin's,
"When will you pay me?" say the bells of Old
　　Bailey,
"When I grow rich," say the bells of
　　Shoreditch,
"When will that be?" say the bells of Stepney,
"I'm sure I don't know," says the great bell of
　　Bow.
Here comes a candle to light you to bed,
Here comes a chopper to chop off your head.

At the words "chop off your head" the 'arch' makes a chopping movement up and down and catches one of the children in the chain. This 'prisoner' is then asked to choose if he wants to be an orange or lemon. (The other children should not hear his choice.) He then joins on behind the leader of his own side. When all the children have been caught, the two teams have a tug-of-war.

Yoghurt and lemon cookies

¾ cup (150g) unsalted butter
1½ cups (300g) caster sugar
Grated rind of 1 lemon
2 teaspoons lemon juice
2 eggs
2 cups (400g) plain flour
½ cup (100g) cornflour
½ teaspoon bicarbonate of soda
2 tablespoons plain yoghurt

Preheat the oven to 180°C, 350°F, Gas Mark 4.

Grease two baking trays.

Beat the butter, sugar and lemon rind together until light and fluffy. Add the lemon juice and mix well together.

Add the eggs one at a time, beating well and making sure the mixture does not curdle.

Sift the flour, cornflour and soda into the mixture, add the yoghurt and mix well.

Place the mixture in spoonfuls on the baking trays, leaving room for each biscuit to spread.

Bake for 10 – 12 minutes, or until golden. Cool on the trays for 2 – 3 minutes before transferring to a wire rack to cool completely.

For an extra special touch, ice the biscuits with lemon icing made from icing sugar, fresh lemon juice and a few drops of water.

Ambrosia

3 oranges
2 ripe bananas
2 tablespoons chopped dates
2 tablespoons granulated or caster sugar
½ cup (50g) grated or desiccated coconut

Peel the oranges and cut them in pieces into a dish. Add thinly sliced bananas, sugar and the dates.

Sprinkle the grated coconut onto the fruit and chill before serving.

Apricot ice cream

1¾ cups (350g) dried apricots, soaked in water for 2 hours
2 tablespoons lemon juice
3 egg whites
⁷/₈ cup (175g) caster sugar
⁷/₈ cup (200ml) (³/₈ pint) whipped or double cream

Cover the apricots with water and simmer gently for 20 minutes.

Drain, reserving ½ cup (125ml) (¼ pint) of the liquid.

Cool slightly, then blend the apricots, liquid and lemon juice on maximum speed for 30 seconds. Cool completely.

Whisk the egg whites until stiff, then gradually whisk in the sugar.

Fold the apricot purée with the cream into the sugar and egg mixture.

Turn into a freezerproof container, cover, seal and freeze until solid.

Transfer from the freezer to the fridge at least 10 minutes before serving.

Tropical surprise

½ mango
Juice of 1 small orange
Juice of 1 lime
3 tablespoons white rum
2 ice cubes
½ cup (115ml) soda water
Orange or lemon slices to decorate, or sprigs of lemon balm

Peel the mango and chop the flesh. Blend with the fruit juices, rum and ice cubes on maximum speed for 30 seconds.

Divide the mango mixture between glasses and top up with soda water. Decorate with fruit slices or sprigs of lemon balm.

For a special effect you can dip the tops of the glasses in beaten egg white then in caster sugar before pouring in the drinks.

Banana fizz

1 banana
1 slice pineapple
Juice of ½ lemon
1 tablespoon caster sugar
½ cup (115ml) lemonade
Crushed ice to serve

Put all the ingredients except the lemonade in a blender and blend on maximum speed for 30 seconds.

Strain the mixture into a jug and stir in the lemonade.

Serve in glasses half filled with crushed ice.

4. MOONLIGHT NIGHTS

Moonlight nights

Have you ever driven across an unlit country road after dark? Or could you possibly imagine life before electricity? Well I can. I grew up in a village on the small Caribbean island of Dominica (not the Dominican Republic). There, tropical night would descend thick and fast, enveloping the village in a cloak of velvet darkness. Frogs, crickets and cicadas took this as cue to start up a shrill dusk chorus, noisy and persistent, lasting throughout the night. Millions of shimmering fireflies would also come alive performing a hypnotic dance in accompaniment to the music of the insects.

Humans, however, had other ideas. Without bright lights to lessen the gloom they would go to bed early, quite soon after sunset in fact. When there was moonlight, now that was quite a different story.

Messiers Crick? Crack!
North and South
Mouth open, story jump out
All Hell break loose
And the Devil and his wife about.

In other words, villages bathed all over in pale fluorescent light would come alive with human activity and stay awake till long after sundown.

Everyone, young and old, enjoyed an extra hour or two before bedtime in relaxed and usually jovial mood. While the grown-ups chatted, squatting on doorsteps, perched on benches or logs in the yard or lounged in easy chairs on the verandah, the children played hide-and-seek and various clapping and ring games which I remember as "moonlight games". Some of the games had their origins on distant shores as far away as America; others travelled from neighbouring Caribbean islands. Many were influenced by Europeans, in particular French, English and Spanish. They were all weird and wonderful and in the universal tradition of children's rhymes could effortlessly defy logic, as in:

Down to the carpet you must go
Like a blackbird in the air
Rise and stand up on your knees
And choose the one you love the best
Oh, when you marry, you tell me so
First the boy, second the girl
Sunday after Sunday school
Kiss, Kiss and say goodbye.

or:

Little Sally Water
Sitting in a saucer
Rise Sally rise and wipe your eyes
Sally turn to the east, Sally turn to the west
Sally turn to the very one you love best.

or:

> *Three white horses in the stable*
> *Hey, hey we go up tomorrow*
> *Up tomorrow at break of day*
> *Come along with your shadow play*
> *Shadow play is a ripe banana*
> *Hey, hey we go up tomorrow…*

Two of my favourite song games which I always enjoy sharing at my storytelling sessions are *Jane and Louise* and *Susie in the Moonlight*. They are as enthralling and as magical in London schools and libraries today as they were under a Dominican mango tree by moonlight all those years ago.

SUZIE IN THE MOONLIGHT

Traditional

1. Su - zie in the moon - light,__ Su - zie in the dew.

Su - zie ne - ver come back__ un - til the clock strike two.

2. Walk in Suzie, walk in.
Walk in here I say.
Choose the one you love the best and
Hear the banjo play.

3. I love nobody and
Nobody loves me.
The only one is (—————) so
Come and dance with me.

4. Tra-la-la-la-la-la-la
La-la-la-la-la
Tra-la-la-la-la-la-la
La-la-la-la-la

Suzie in the moonlight

This singing game is traditional throughout the Windward Islands. Suzie's original name in Trinidad was Gypsy but is often called Tootsie, Dootsie and Lucy.

Formation:

Circle of any number of players. Hands at side free to clap. One player outside is Suzie.

Movements:

1. During verse one, players point to Suzie standing outside "in da moonlight."
2. At "walk in" — Suzie walks into the ring.
3. Suzie sings "I love nobody..." by herself and chooses a player.
4. Players sing "Tra-la-la" while Suzie dances with the child she chose. Then that child goes outside the ring to be the next Suzie.

JANE AND LOUISA

Traditional

1. Jane and Lou-i-sa will soon come in, will soon come in, will soon come in. Jane and Lou-i-sa will soon come in, in-to the beau-ti-ful gar - den.

2. My dear, will you allow me
   To pick a rose, pick a rose.
   Jane and Louisa will soon come in,
   Into the beautiful garden.

3. My dear, will you allow me
   To waltz with you, waltz with you.
   Jane and Louisa will soon come in,
   Into the beautiful garden.

Jane and Louisa

Formation:

Circle, with one outside as 'Jane'.

Movements:

1. During verse one, Jane dances around outside the circle, entering during the last part of the verse.

2. Dancer picks a rose by plucking at the dress of another player.

3. During verse three, Jane chooses a 'rose' and brings 'Louisa' into the centre to dance with her (any simple step).

4. To continue, the new Louisa becomes Jane who starts again outside the circle.

Tales and riddles

Among my most precious memories of those times were the storytelling sessions known as Contes and Tims-Tims (Tales and Riddles). Often a large pot of breadnuts (similar to chestnuts) would sit simmering on the fire after supper while word got round that there was to be a 'Conte' gathering at my aunt's that evening. Sometimes those sessions occurred quite spontaneously with the chance passing of a stranger, the exchange of greetings and news and before you knew it a fully blown conte session to which eavesdropping neighbours like bees to nectar would be irresistibly drawn.

The storyteller would usually warm up with a riddle: "Tim-Tim!" (I'll give you a riddle). The audience would respond, "Bwa sesh!" (Go on then).

The riddles might go something like this:

"D'lo sispan? — Coco"
(Hanging water? — Coconuts)

"D'lo dubut? — Canne"
(standing water? — Sugar cane)

"I send my messenger on an errand, the errand arrives before the messenger. — Someone picking coconuts."

"I send my servant to fetch the doctor. The patient lies dead and buried before the servant reaches the doctor, who is the servant? — Mr Snail."

And so on...

Proverbs which were an integral part of everyday speech also featured among the riddles.

"Chatte pas la, wate Ka baye bal."
When the cats are away the mice play.

"La plie belle en bas la baye."
(With proverbial reference to the Cinderella story.) The most beautiful one is hidden under the wash tub.

Night People

Then there were the blood-curdling, hair-raising tales of the Night People. These night people were supposed to emerge from their nooks and crannies as soon as darkness fell and wreak mischief on humans and land animals alike. They came in various shapes and sizes. There was Soucouyant. She was usually an older woman with the power to shed her human form along with her skin and change into a ball of fire which would shoot through the night sky and be seen for miles around. A sort of vampire, she would suck the blood of her victims. However, if anyone was lucky or brave enough to find the hiding place of Soucouyant's skin and sprinkled it with salt and pepper, that was the end of the witch.

There was Loogaroo, the male counterpart of Soucouyant. He was a man who could change into a hoofed animal, usually a goat, donkey or horse. You would know that Loogaroo had been lurking around when you woke up to find hoofprints outside your door.

There was also the 'dwens' wandering spirits of children who died before baptism. They cried out something pitiful from the depths of the forest in the dead of night. There were also the ordinary wandering spirits better known as Zombies or jumbies, also known as duppies in other parts of the Caribbean. Many a young person would be discouraged from going out to socialize at night with the warning "Mind jumbie don't hold you, you know."

Queen of all the night people had to be Ladiablesse, the she devil. She appeared in the

guise of a mysterious beauty, usually walking along a lonely road, always impeccably dressed in a long black dress to hide her one human foot and one cloven hoof. Men, married and single, were said to lose their heads over Ladiablesse who would meet her revenge by luring them along in her company, leading them to the edge of a precipice, whereupon she suddenly revealed a hideously ugly face complete with chilling, mocking laughter before vanishing. Many a male traveller has been known to die or narrowly escape death at the hands of this sinister lady in black.

Then of course there was Diable, the devil himself who ruled over all the night people. He was more often than not a fair skinned man who rode on a horse sitting in a peculiar back to front position so that a traveller would be confused as to whether the horseman was approaching or going away.

These night people as far as everyone was concerned *were* real. One of them could indeed be one's next door neighbour (Soucouyant and Loogaroo were ordinary humans by day). Others at one time or another would have been seen by someone's grandmother or accosted one's great uncle when he was a brave but foolish young man out at dead of night courting his woman from the village over the river.

Listening to the exploits of the Night People was an occasion never to be missed even though it meant not being able to go to bed unless huddled up close to a grown up and even if it guaranteed bad dreams for many nights to come.

Jane Grell.

5. TANABATA

Tanabata festival

The meeting of the two lovers (7th July).

When I think about a Japanese festival that I would like to share with my non-Japanese friends, Tanabata is the one that most readily springs to mind. For me, it is the least complicated of Japanese festivals both in the manner of its celebration and its ritual significance; perhaps as a result, it also seems to be the most ephemeral of all festivities. I remember it as a time of fun and magic. In recounting my childhood memories of Tanabata, I have the impression that I have compressed my experiences of several Tanabata festivals into one.

Tanabata is celebrated on the 7th July when summer seems to be at its hottest and stickiest. And it is celebrated in the evening.

As I remember, there was very little preparation during the day. At the most, there might be a freshly cut bamboo tree with its dry leaves rustling in the wind; it would be put near the house in the garden. After supper, my family (my parents and a brother) would take a cooling bath. Then we would don our yukata (a very casual version of kimono that is worn in summer, typically after a bath) and step out into the garden. We would tie strips of coloured paper, cut out paper decorations and origami, and small bells that chime with the wind onto the bamboo branches; some of these strips of paper had poems or some saying written on them.

Once we had finished decorating, we would light fireworks. We would hold on to the small sparklers and draw circles of light that vanished

as quickly as they were drawn. After a while the garden would be suffused with the smell of sulphur. The fire rockets were handled by my father. We children were solemnly told to keep a good distance from him lest the rockets exploded on the ground — they never did.

In between the fireworks and the decoration of the bamboo tree, my mother would tell us the story of the two lovers.

In the Heavens (Chinese to be precise), there lived a cowherd and a weaver, each busying themselves working for the gods. One day, they met and fell in love. They were so much in love with each other that they spent all their time together. And they forgot their task.

Soon the gods were running out of cloths to make clothes out of, they were also short on milk and meat. Casting around for the cause of this inconvenient shortage, the gods found the two lovers oblivious to the world. The gods separated the two by putting them one on each side of the heavenly river, the Milky Way. Thus separated, the two lovers returned to their task.

One tended to his cattle and the other wove; but as they did so, they wept bitterly at their separation.

Seeing them suffer so, the gods took pity. The gods agreed that the two lovers should be allowed to cross the Milky Way once a year to be together. The day of their brief but regular reunion is 7th July, Tanabata.

In Japan we celebrate this reunion with paper decorations and fireworks.

In Tokyo, spectacular fireworks are shot into the sky above the River Sumida. During the Edo period (seventeenth to nineteenth century), this firework show was a competition between two large and well-known firework stores. Every time there was a firework display, the citizens of Edo who had gathered around the river to cool themselves and enjoy the spectacle would call out the name of the store in support.

In Sendai, a city in Northern Honshu, Tanabata is celebrated a month later (more in keeping with the lunar calendar which we used till the latter half of the nineteenth century). The city is famous for the very ornate paper decorations (some might weigh almost a ton) and puppet shows that can be seen in shopping malls.

Quite a few towns and cities have their own celebration of Tanabata; but they are not well known like the two cities I have just mentioned.

I remember one Tanabata evening when we children quickly donned our Yukata and with our fans handy we walked up a cliff with our parents. We fanned ourselves busily warding off the mosquitoes. All the time I kept on staring at the sky and sea. Looking down, the dark sea slithered into the beach with white horses dancing around jutting rocks. Very frequently, it would light up with flashes of reds and yellows. For above us in the skies large red and yellow chrysanthemum flowers were blossoming, and their petals were cascading down into darkness.

Coming home still excited with this spectacle, I remember looking up into the sky. My mother had pointed out the Milky Way to us. As I stared, I thought of two lovers who were reunited but for a while before being separated yet again.

Haruko Kinase-Leggett.

The tale of the weaving maid and the cowherd

In China many tales are told about the stars and the heavens. During the seventh month, the days are hot and nights are clear. If you look into the sky on the night of the seventh day of the seventh night — known as the Double Seventh Night — it is said that it is possible to see two figures walking over a rushing river across a bridge spanned by magpies. The river is what we know as the Milky Way. The two figures are known as a Heavenly Maid and a Cowherd, and their story, told below, is popular throughout China.

Those who are lucky will be able to see the scene and if they do, and kneel down immediately to pray for wealth, a long life or a son, one of these wishes will come true within three years! It is also said that, when the figures are crossing the bridge, the gates of heaven are wide open, and if someone picks up a brick and throws it into the sky the brick will turn to gold as it falls back down.

Many hundreds of years ago, when the mighty Ming Emperors ruled over China, there was also a very powerful Emperor in heaven. He had a beautiful daughter who spent all her days busily spinning and weaving, her nimble fingers scarcely pausing as she made heavenly garments out of cloudy silk. Because her father was the

Heavenly Emperor, she was sometimes allowed to leave the heavens and go down to earth, accompanied by six other young girls from heaven. They would all go down together to play and bathe in the silvery waters of a magnificent river.

A poor cowherd lived near the river. He was an orphan, and had lived for many years with his elder brother and his brother's wife. He worked hard on his brother's land, doing more than his fair share of the work, but his brother's wife did not like him, and one day she finally forced him to leave their house. He took with him nothing but a broken cart and an ancient ox, and was given two acres of barren land beside the river. Cowherd never complained, but relied on his old ox to help him to earn a meagre living. He was fond of his ox, and called him 'Elder Brother the Ox'.

Now, Elder Brother the Ox felt sorry for poor Cowherd who was honest and good and worked very hard for little reward, and he decided to help Cowherd to find a wife. Ox told Cowherd that, on a certain night, seven fairy girls would come down to the river to play and bathe. If he managed to take the cloth from any one of these girls, she would marry him.

So one misty moonlit night soon afterwards, Cowherd crept down to the river. He was entranced by the beautiful girls and he managed to bring home the cloth belonging to one of them, the Emperor's daughter, the Weaving Maid. Sure enough, Weaving Maid agreed straightaway to marry him, and the two of them became very deeply in love. For three years they lived together in great happiness, and they had two children.

But when the Emperor of Heaven found out that his daughter was living as Cowherd's wife he was furious. He sent her grandmother, the Queen Mother of the Western Heaven, down to earth to bring Weaving Maid back to the heavens, and she was prevented from ever returning to earth. Both Heavenly Maid and Cowherd were terribly unhappy, for it seemed impossible for Cowherd ever to find a way to heaven, and his wife could never return to earth.

Elder Brother the Ox could not bear to see his master so unhappy, so he broke off one of his horns and used his special powers to make it into a boat. Cowherd and his children got into this boat and were able to soar through the clouds up to the heavens. It was a long journey, but Cowherd eventually spotted his lovely wife. He was just about to catch up with her when he was seen by the Queen Mother of the Western Heaven. She immediately took a gold pin from her hair and drew a line with it across the heavens, a line which turned into a rushing river in the sky. Neither Cowherd nor Weaving Maid could cross its fierce water, they could only look at each other across it.

The Phœnix was the leader of all the birds in the sky. He became friendly with both Cowherd and Weaving Maid, and wanted to help them because he saw that they loved each other so much. He called all the magpies in the universe together, and asked them to help the couple and make a bridge over the river. On the seventh day of the seventh month the magpies all joined up and made an arched bridge in the heavens, and the couple were able to cross the river and reunite once more.

6. RAKSHA BANDHAN

Raksha Bandhan festival

Although Raksha Bandhan is a Hindu festival it is celebrated by many Indians, whatever their religion. Many Sikh families follow the custom of giving rakhi.

Raksha Bandhan is celebrated in August. On the day, sisters tie a rakhi onto their brothers' wrists. The rakhi is a sign of affection between a brother and sister. When a sister ties one onto her brother's wrist, it means that she trusts him to protect and look after her. She says a prayer asking God to keep her brother safe. In return the brother often gives a small gift to his sister. It may be a flower, sweets or some money, and he promises to look after her. Raksha means protect, bandhan is to tie.

Just before Raksha Bandhan many Indian shops are full of colourful glittering rakhi. A rakhi is a bracelet made of red and gold coloured thread or braid which is twisted or plaited. The rakhi can include shiny or glittery materials and may have a decorative medallion at the centre of it.

Raksha Bandhan is not just a festival for children. As adults, sisters will give or send a rakhi to their brothers and will take a gift of homemade sweets or cakes. In return a brother will give a gift to his sister; it may be a new sari.

A rakhi is symbolic of binding a brother and sister together forever. There may be family disputes and brothers and sisters can stop being friends but they can't ever stop being brother and sister.

Raksha Bandhan cards

Girls might like to make cards for their brothers, father or an adopted brother for the day. The card could be decorated and include a simple verse. An example from a Raksha Bandhan card is written below.

Make up your own verse, girls, to tell your brother how much you really love him.

> On this Raksha Bandhan Day
> I send you a Rakhi and firmly pray
> May the glowing Rakhi
> Which adorns your wrist today
> Light your heart with joy and hope
> And with love that's strong and true
> May it brighten all your days
> Bringing health and strength to you
> God bless you — my dear brother.

Boys, don't forget to have a little gift ready for your sister.

Make a Rakhi

A Rakhi:

A Rakhi for Mere Pyare Bhaiya:

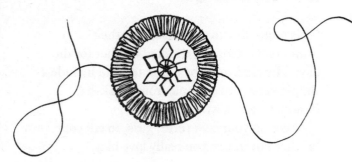

Use red and gold thread or braid. Decorate with shiny and glittering materials and beads.

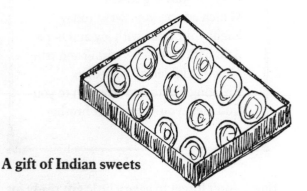

A gift of Indian sweets

225g desiccated coconut
100g icing sugar
200g small can condensed milk
Food colouring

Mix all the ingredients together. Roll into walnut sized balls. Coat with icing sugar and leave to set.

If the ingredients are doubled, half the sweets can be coloured with red food colouring and the other half with yellow or green. When dry the sweets can be arranged in a box lined with a gold doyley to make them look really special. Cling film over the top of an open box will prevent the sweets from drying out too much.

How the world began

This is one of the oldest Hindu creation stories. In this story, Lord Brahma is the Creator. While he sleeps, nothing exists, but when he wakes he creates the universe. This happens over and over again, in a never-ending cycle.

Before the world began, there was only a lotus flower floating on a sea of milk. Within its creamy, magical petals God himself, Lord Brahma, lay sleeping peacefully.

He had been sleeping for more than eternity. While he was asleep the universe could not exist; but as his eyelids opened, there was a trembling over the endless milky surface of the sea. Lord Brahma awoke, and life began once more.

Lord Brahma looked around and saw how lonely he was. He was so lonely that he wept. Great tears rolled down his cheeks. Some fell into the sea and became the earth. Others he brushed away and they became the air and sky. Then he stretched. He stretched upwards and his body became the universe, and outwards to create day and night. He stretched and created twilight and moonlight; fire, wind and rain. He created the dry seasons and the wet seasons, and then he created the gods.

The gods of darkness were called Asuras. Their friends were demons, goblins, giants and serpents.

The gods of light were called Devas. They shone with beauty and goodness, and their friends were fairies, nymphs, angels and saints.

In the sea of milk was a miraculous element called amrit. Anyone who drank it stayed young forever. The Devas wanted to get the amrit out of the ocean and keep it for themselves. The Asuras too wanted to get the amrit out of the ocean and keep it for themselves. But the only way to get it was by churning the sea of milk, and neither the Devas nor the Asuras could manage that alone. Enemies as they were, they had to work together.

To churn the ocean, they needed a churning rod and rope. But what rod and rope could they

find, powerful enough to churn the sea of milk?

They came to a great mountain which rose out of the sea. It was the mountain Mandrachal. "This is the churning rod!" cried the Devas.

The Asuras came with a monstrous serpent, long and winding, with a hooded head and darting tongue. "This is our rope," they said. They wound the serpent round the mountain. Then the Asuras took hold of the serpent's terrible head, and the Devas grasped his long, thrashing tail. Between them they began to tug to and fro, to and fro. The mountain began to churn the sea. The ocean of milk began to froth and foam. Steam poured from the serpent's mouth. Lightning flashed. Fire and rain swirled about. Still they heaved this way and that, until at last the sea of milk was one great whirlpool. It began to turn to butter, and at last, there was the precious amrit glistening in the thickening waves.

Suddenly an angel came flying over the ocean carrying a golden goblet. He swooped down, and filled it with amrit.

The Devas and Asuras rushed towards the angel, ready to fight for the amrit. But the great God did not want the Asuras to have the amrit, lest the demons should have too much power.

Then one of the demons disguised himself as a Deva. Standing between the sun and moon, he reached out. The angel gave him the golden goblet. Immediately he tipped back his head and drank.

The sun and moon saw this. "Stop!" they cried.

"That is the terrible demon, Rahu!" The magic liquid was just trickling down Rahu's throat, when the God of all struck off his head. The body plunged downwards, dead, but because the amrit had reached his throat, the head could live for ever. It soared up into the sky, roaring and howling.

The Devas and the Asuras flew at each other in fury. A fearful battle began. Burning rocks and mountains, thunderbolts and fiery arrows flew through the sky. But the Devas were more powerful. Gradually the Asuras and demons were defeated. Thousands lay dead and dying, while others crawled away to hide in the bowels of the earth, and the caverns of the sea.

Of all the demons, only Rahu's head would live for ever. His gaping mouth chased the sun and the moon around the heavens. If he caught one and swallowed it, there was an eclipse, but only until it slipped through his throat and out into the sky again.

Jamila Gavin.

7. MAWLID AN-NABI

Birthday of the Prophet

"Muhammad was born on the morning of the 12th *Rabi'al-Awwal*, the third month of the Muslim calendar, corresponding to 20th August 570AD. Coincidentally, he also died on the same day, sixty-three years later. For Muslims, the birth of the prophet is one of the most important events in the history of the world. Not only was he the last of the prophets, he was also the receiver of the Qur'an, which contains the code of life by which all Muslims live."

M M Ahsan, *Muslim Festivals*, Wayland (Publishers) Ltd. 1985.

In many communities, Muhammad's birthday is celebrated with street processions leading to the mosque for worship followed by a special meal. It is a joyful time of appreciation. Stories of the prophet's life are told; his tasks, his character, his mission and the eventual establishment of Islam. One favourite story concerns the Ka'ba, the sacred, cube-like building in Mecca known as the 'House of God' and constructed some 4,000 years ago by Abraham. Muslims face this building and Mecca when they pray:

It happened once, long ago, that great floods damaged the Ka'ba. At that time Muhammad was a young boy who willingly helped with repairs and rebuilding. When the large sacred black stone had been mended there was a dispute then who would put it back in its place. Each leader and chief in the land wanted the honour of replacing it and heated arguments broke out! Finally one elderly, wise man suggested that they should stop their quarrelling and leave the matter until the following morning. Then they could put their question to the first man to enter the Kaaba.

As it happened, Muhammad was the first to enter the next morning. The chiefs agreed to accept his word, for they considered him to be trustworthy. Indeed, he had this as a nickname, 'the trustworthy.' Muhammad asked for a large sheet which he laid on the ground. In the middle of it he placed the black stone. Then he told the chiefs of each tribe to take hold of the sheet and slowly raise it to the height where the stone was to be replaced. Gently it was slid into place from the sheet, and all felt that they had shared in the honourable task. So Muhammad's way had been fair and just, and avoided further fighting!

PRAYER TO THE PROPHET MUHAMMAD

(Verses 2 to 4 translated from Bengali by Alam and Chowdhury)

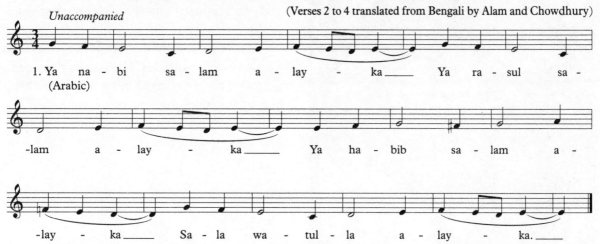

Unaccompanied

1. Ya na-bi sa-lam a-lay - ka___ Ya ra-sul sa-
(Arabic)

-lam a-lay - ka___ Ya ha-bib sa-lam a-

-lay - ka___ Sa-la wa-tul-la a-lay - ka.

2. For the sun and moon shine in the sky,
   But that light does not shine bright enough
   And my heart is filled with light from you
   Like a new sun in the sky of my mind.

3. With your light divine the world is awake,
   And the nightingale is singing again;
   See the flowers have started blossoming
   And the world is filled with light and joy.

4. I am not a prophet — only a child,
   Not an angel nor a prophet of God,
   So I give my thanks to God because
   He has made me one of your followers.

The Feast of the One Hundred Camels

Here is another story, written as told by Muhammad's grandfather to the young boy. (See the festival of Eid story.)

"And now, I shall tell you about the Feast of the One Hundred Camels. What a noble beast the camel is! How valuable to the Arab people, think of it! What animal can go for twenty-five days without water? Why, a man under such circumstances would have perished long before the twentieth!

"Now tell me, my little man who once lived with the Bedouin, how did they cook their meals and heat their bodies on cold desert nights?"

Abd al-Muttalib turned to the elders then, and proceeded with his story in a deep but quiet voice.

"After this boy's father was born, I was faced with an awful reminder. I had made a pledge to God, and the time had come for it to be fulfilled. Perhaps some of you remember that night? Indeed, how could anyone forget who had been present at the time?

"The air was so still as to be stifling. The shadows sharp and unrelenting before the sacrificial altar where my sons and I had gathered. Surely, they must have foreseen a sombre event, yet they did not hold back. I told them about the pledge — that when I was still young and searching fervently for the well of Zam-Zam, I made a promise to God, if he would give me 10 sons to grow to maturity to help me with my work, that I would sacrifice one of them near the Ka'ba... how proud a father I was in the secret of my heart, when they all consented. Then, you remember, the arrows of chance were drawn, and his name... my beloved 'Abdullah's name... was called out.

"Ah, my heart turned to ice within my breast. Yet, girding up my courage and will I clasped my young son by the hand and led him, with determined steps, to the sacrificial altar. It was at that instant... do you remember?... that cries of compassion arose and a voice proclaimed 'Hold! Father of 'Abdullah, stay your hand! This cannot be!'

Before Muhammad had a chance to answer this question and the others that followed, his grandfather had answered them himself and gone on with the story.

"Why, they used camel's dung for fuel and heat," continued his grandfather. "And what did someone discover long ago, when his skin bag full of camel's milk had been shaken up on a long trek across the desert? Why, cheese, of course! And what is the tastiest meat of all, after a long day's journey? The meat of a camel, well roasted until tender. And what, tell me, is used to make the best tents? A camel hide. And this is his last offering to man. Without the camel, no one would be able to survive in this country of deserts. So that is why, you see, my little one, a camel's life according to tradition, may be worth the life of a man".

"I turned, stunned and confused to face the assembly. The men of the Quraysh were gathered in fervent consultation.

"'We have decided,' they announced, 'to consult the sorceress of Madina... and we are off to see her now!'

"Well, two long days went by before the answer came. And again we gathered between the sacrificial idols, while the decision of the sorceress was announced:

'One arrow shall be for ten camels, the other arrow with the name of your son. Ten camels shall equal the life of your son. If the arrow drawn is that of your son, then multiply the number of camels, and draw again... keep drawing until God is satisfied.'

"Again and again we threw the arrows until finally the camel's arrow was drawn, and the number of camels to be sacrificed was 100. With tears on my cheeks and thanks in my heart I embraced my young son.

"What great rejoicing there was in the city that night! One hundred camels were sacrificed, and we prepared a huge feast. All the citizens of Makka, down to the very poorest, were given a generous share: it was said that even the little beasts of the desert partook of the scraps. And until this day, no one — and I'm sure none of you were present — has ever forgotten the Feast of the One Hundred Camels."

The lights of the Ka'ba were growing dim. Abd al-Muttalib gathered up his grandson in his huge, warm cloak, while the others took leave of him and made their way home through the dark, and narrow winding streets.

Those who had just listened to the tale did not dream — nor did anyone else in Makka at that time — that 'Abdullah of the One Hundred Camels had indeed served God's purpose; not as a sacrifice but as the father of Muhammad, God's Messenger, later to be called the Last of the Prophets.

Mardijah A Tarantino.

A dinner of smells

Nasrudin the mullah (teacher) is a well-known character in many Muslim stories. Although he sometimes appears to be foolish, he is really very wise.

On the corner of a busy street in a bustling market town there once stood a very fine restaurant, where delicious dishes were prepared for wealthy customers.

One day a poor man was walking through the town. He was very hungry for he hadn't eaten all day, and he stopped outside the restaurant to sniff the wonderful smells wafting out from the delicious food inside. After a few moments he smiled sadly, and walked on.

He had not gone more than a few steps when the restaurant owner rushed out. He was a very rich man, who had not become rich through being generous and he called out: "Stop, thief! I saw you! You have taken the smell of my food and you must pay for it!"

The poor man did not know what he could do. He had no money. "I have nothing to pay you with!" he stammered.

"We'll see about that!" shouted the restaurant owner. "You are coming with me to the Qadi!"

A Qadi is a judge in a Muslim court, and the poor man was terrified because the Qadi was a powerful figure.

The Qadi heard the story: "This is rather an unusual tale," he said, "I shall have to go away and think what should be done. Come back here in the morning."

The poor man went back to his humble room, but he could not sleep that night. He knew that he couldn't pay anything, whatever the Qadi decided, and he worried all night long. In the morning he got up, feeling quite miserable, and when he had said his prayers he went along to the Qadi's house.

On the way he spied Nasrudin the mullah. Nasrudin was said to be a clever man, and a good one, so the poor man went up to him and told him the whole story. Nasrudin said that he would come to the court to speak up for him.

The rich restaurant owner had got there before them, and he was already chatting to the Qadi. When the poor man saw that the two of them were friends he was more worried than ever, sure that the judgement would be against him.

Sure enough, the Qadi almost immediately began to insult the poor man, calling him all manner of rude names, and ordered him to pay a large sum of money to the rich restaurant owner.

At once Nasrudin stepped forward. "My Lord," he said to the Qadi, "This man is my brother. Please allow me to pay instead of him." Then the mullah took a soft leather bag full of coins from his belt, and held it next to the rich man's ear.

"Can you hear the money?" he asked, as he jingled the coins together inside the bag.

"Of course I can," the man replied impatiently.

"Then you have had your payment," said the mullah. "My brother has smelt your food, and you have heard his money. The debt is paid."

There could be no disputing such an argument, so the case was settled and the poor man went free.

---

8. JANMASHTAMI

Krishna Janmashtami

Janmashtami falls on the eighth day of Shravan which comes between August and September. It is the festival to celebrate the birth of Lord Krishna the eighth incarnation of God. Krishna was born at midnight so the celebrations begin at midnight.

At the Shree Ram Mandir in Birmingham, I left my shoes in the foyer at 11.15pm, before entering the prayer hall where a buzz of excitement and expectation met me at the door. The hall was crowded with small children, teenagers, parents and grandparents sitting on chairs or on the floor talking, listening to the Indian music; watching and waiting. Many of the adults had fasted all day before coming to the Mandir to see the re-enactment of Vashudeva taking the newly born Krishna to safety.

At 11.30 the heavy curtains were closed in front of the shrine figures. The curtains then provided a back-drop for Krishna's cradle which was hidden under a golden fabric.

Young children passed among the people distributing rose petals and rice from large bowls. The excitement grew and at about 11.45 everyone formed two lines representing the river Yamuna. The back doors of the mandir opened and a young man dressed as Vasudeva came in carrying a brass figure of baby Krishna in a basket.

Curved around the back of the basket was the many headed cobra which provided the protective shield over Krishna.

As Vasudeva walked slowly through the river of people carrying Krishna above his head, arms were waved to indicate the rough water and rose petals and rice were thrown towards the baby Krishna.

At midnight, the exact moment of Krishna's birth, the conch shell was blown and the curtains opened. The cover was taken from the cradle joyfully and everyone took part in a special Arti ceremony.

Happiness and laughter filled the air as rice, petals, red powder and a milky substance was liberally sprinkled over everyone. A long line of devotees was formed in front of Krishna's cradle; as individuals reached the cradle it was rocked to amuse baby Krishna, prayers were said to him and a money offering was made. Prashad consisting of milky sweets and a handful of nuts, seeds, dried fruits and sugar crystal was received by the devotees as they left the cradle; for many this broke the fast.

Children and adults went home in a festive mood, the children to go to bed and the parents to eat dishes made from yoghurt, milk and honey to complete the Janmashtami celebration.

The story of Krishna's birth

Once, long ago, a cruel and wicked man called Kansa was told by a voice from the sky that the eighth child of his sutor Devaki and her husband Vasudeva would kill him. Kansa was so angry that his newly married sister's son would kill him that he threw Devaki and Vasudeva into prison. The prison was heavily guarded night and day so there was no way for them to escape. Over the years, every time a baby was born to Devaki it was taken away from her by the guards. This happened seven times. The eighth time Devaki's eighth baby was born in the middle of the night at exactly midnight. Bright stars shone in the sky that night and everyone knew that something special had happened.

Vasudeva wrapped up his newly born baby son and put him carefully into a basket. He tried the cell door which was unlocked and stepped outside. To his amazement all the guards were sound asleep so Vasudeva was able to carry baby Krishna out of the prison to a place of safety. He knew of a cowherd and his wife called Nanda and Yasoda whom he could trust to raise the baby Krishna as one of their own children.

It became a stormy night and Vasudeva had to cross a deep and quickly flowing river to get to the cowherd's house. It is said that when baby Krishna's toe touched the rising water the river became still and Vasudeva could cross quite easily. The baby Krishna had also been protected from the storm by a many headed cobra who rose up out of the water to shield him from the torrential rain.

After Vasudeva had safely carried Krishna to Nanda and Yasoda he went back to his wife in prison without being detected.

Krishna grew up as Yasoda's son. There are many stories of the naughty tricks he got up to when he teased the milkmaids so that he could steal their butter and cream. Krishna loved to eat butter.

As he grew older Yasoda realized that she did not have to worry about Krishna's safety as he proved himself to be a very special little boy. The prophecy of the voice from the sky came true when Krishna destroyed the evil Kansa and became and honest and fair ruler in his place.

Recipes for Janmashtami

As a child, Krishna loved butter and cream so much that whenever he had the opportunity he would creep into the dairy and steal some.

To make butter.

Screw topped jar
Glass marble
Full cream milk

Fill the screw topped jar with full cream milk. Add the glass marble and screw the top tightly onto the jar. Shake the jar vigorously. The marble will increase the friction inside the jar and the butter will form more quickly. When the butter has formed in the jar, pour off the excess liquid from the milk and remove the marble.

To make sweet butters.

Try these recipes for sugar'n'spice butter and choc'n'nut flavoured butter.

Sugar'n'spice.

100g butter
15ml (1 level tablespoon) brown sugar
15ml (1 level tablespoon) ground cinnamon.

Thoroughly beat the butter, sugar, and cinnamon together. Sugar'n'spice is delicious on hot toast waffles or drop scones.

Choc'n'nut butter.

100g butter
10ml (2 level teaspoons) castor sugar
15ml (1 level tablespoon) grated chocolate
30ml (2 level tablespoons) chopped walnuts.

Beat all the ingredients together thoroughly. Choc'n'nut butter makes a scrumptious filling for hot pancakes or a spread on hot toast.

Semolina and almond halva.

100g butter
100g fine semolina
100g ground almonds
100g sugar
½ teaspoon ground nutmeg
300ml full cream milk
25g unsalted cashew nuts, chopped

Grease a baking tray. Melt the butter over a low heat in a heavy-based pan. Add the semolina. Stir continuously and cook until it is golden brown. Stir in the almonds, sugar and nutmeg. Add the milk and stir until the mixture thickens and stops sticking to the pan. Spread the mixture evenly over the baking tray. Sprinkle the chopped cashew nuts evenly over the top and press down into the mixture with a wooden spoon.

When the mixture is cool, cut it into 2cm squares. The halva is a filling, delicious treat chosen for Janmashtami because it is a milk based sweet.

How Ganesh got his elephant head

Also celebrated in August-September, is the birth of Ganesh, the much loved Hindu elephant god.

Shiva, the mighty god with the blue throat, lives up in the Himalaya Mountains with his beautiful wife, Parvati. Sometimes, life is not much fun for her, for Shiva is often away for years at a time on his usual business of creating and destroying people and dancing on top of the world to keep it going.

On one occasion Parvati did not know when he might return. She was bored. There was not much she could do all by herself on a mountain peak, and she was feeling exceedingly lonely. It suddenly occurred to her that she was, after all, a goddess and could do whatever she wished. What she needed was a playmate… not a playmate that would annoy Shiva, as his anger could be deadly in more senses than one, but a sweet, innocent playmate… Parvati kept thinking along these lines. Finally, the perfect solution dawned on her.

"I will make myself a baby," she cried with happiness, "I will make myself a baby boy."

Parvati found some clay and water. She pounded the clay until it was soft and pliable and then she began to shape a baby. The first form she made looked too ordinary and not cuddly enough. So she began to add clay to its

stomach until it was fat and round. Parvati laughed to herself. She was beginning to love the baby already.

Parvati then took her right forefinger and poked it into the baby's stomach to make a belly button. "Oh, it is going to be a lovely baby," she said to herself.

She put the baby in the sun to dry. Soon it opened its eyes and began to smile. Parvati was overjoyed. She had found the perfect playmate.

Everywhere Parvati went, she took her baby. She cooed to it, talked to it and spent many hours laughing at its antics.

Several years passed this way. One day, Parvati took her son for a long walk. They were both quite tired and when they came to a pool of water Parvati wanted to stop and bathe in it, but she felt shy about being seen by a passerby. So she said to her son, "Could you please be my guard? Don't let anyone come near the pool while I am bathing." The roly-poly boy sat down upon a large flat stone while his mother made her way into the refreshing water.

Now, it so happened that Shiva had just finished dancing on a mountain top and was returning home. He heard some splashing in a pool and knew that it had to be his wife. He was about to walk towards the water when he found himself stopped by a fat little boy.

"Don't go any further," the boy ordered.

Shiva was not used to taking orders. He tried to brush the boy aside but the boy resisted and fought back. Shiva's anger began to mount. His throat became bluer and the veins in his forehead began to swell and throb. Suddenly, without warning, Shiva drew out a sword and cut off the boy's head.

Parvati, heard a commotion, slipped into her clothes and rushed towards her son. She let out a scream and fell sobbing to the ground.

Shiva watched in amazement. He realized that he had done something terrible but did not know what it was. He apologized, hoping that would calm his wife, and then asked her what he had done to upset her so.

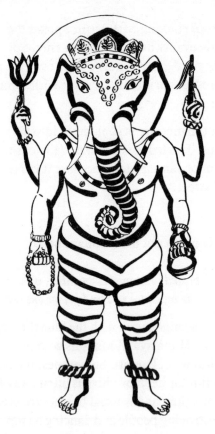

"It's your vile temper," she answered.

"But," he said, "you knew about my temper when you married me. Surely that is not what is upsetting you now!"

"You have murdered our child." Parvati was quite hysterical by now.

"Our child?" asked Shiva. This was the first he had heard of a child.

"You never understand anything," Parvati screamed. "You stay away for years and years on distant mountain tops. You don't care what happens to me."

Shiva did not seem to understand.

"You said that I had killed our child. But we have no child!"

"Of course we have," Parvati said. "We have a child because I made one. I made one because I was lonely. I was lonely because you were away. Of course we have a child. I should say that... we... *had*... a... child."

The pieces in the puzzle suddenly locked into place. Shiva was so sorry that he begged his wife to tell him what he could do to redeem himself.

Parvati said, "Go out into the forest with your mighty sword. I want you to cut off the head of the first living creature you see and bring it back. Fit the head on our child and give it life. That is what I want. If you do not do this for me, I will never speak to you again."

Even though Shiva's work took him away for long periods, he did love his wife and did not want to lose her. So he did as he was told. He went into the forest with his mighty sword, looking for a living creature.

Well, the first living creature he saw was an elephant. Shiva cut off its head and dutifully brought it home. He fitted the head on to the child's body, breathing life into it as he did so, and waited for his wife's reaction.

To his surprise, Parvati was enchanted. She stroked the child's trunk and declared that this boy was even better than her first creation.

Shiva sighed with relief. By now, he was beginning to get very fond of the child himself...

Shiva and Parvati named their son 'Ganesh'.

Madhur Jaffrey.

9. MORE SUMMER FOOD

Kulfi (Indian ice cream)

This is a very rich hard textured ice cream. Traditionally made in long tin moulds with closely fitting lids, you can also use plastic ice cube trays or other shallow containers.

Atul kela (banana) kulfi.

10 cups (2.25l) (4 pints) creamy milk
½ cup (100g) sugar
1 cup (100g) flaked almonds
1 cup (100g) grated pistachio nuts
2 ripe bananas, peeled and chopped
1 teaspoon coarsely ground green cardamom
  seeds
2 teaspoons rose water

Put the milk in a deep pan and bring to the boil. Add the sugar, almonds and pistachios and leave to simmer on a low heat until the milk is reduced by half. Stir from time to time to make sure the milk doesn't boil over.

Remove the pan from the heat and add the banana and cardamom. Let the milk cool to blood heat and then pour it into clean shallow plastic containers. Ideally, the containers should have lids, but you can cover them with tin foil. Place the containers in the freezer for at least 1 hour, then the kulfi should be frozen. To serve, cut the kulfi into slices and sprinkle generously with rose water.

Royal kulfi

3¾ cups (900ml) (1½ pints) creamy milk
1 cup (225ml) sweetened condensed milk
1 cup (200g) sugar
½ cup (50g) flaked almonds
¼ cup (25g) chopped pistachios
1 cup (175g) diced peaches, pears and
   pineapple (fresh or canned)
1 teaspoon green cardamom powder
2 teaspoons rose water
¼ cup grated pistachios

Put the milk in a deep pan and bring to the boil.
Leave it to simmer over a low heat for about 20
minutes, stirring occasionally to make sure it
doesn't boil over. Add the condensed milk,
then the sugar, almonds and chopped
pistachios. Mix well together and leave on the
low heat for 15 minutes, stirring occasionally.

Remove the pan from the heat and leave to cool
to blood heat. Add the fruit, having first
drained any syrup, and the cardamom powder.
Mix carefully and pour the mixture into shallow
plastic containers, preferably with lids.

Freeze for at least one hour until the kulfi is
solid. Before serving, decorate with grated
pistachios and transfer to the fridge for 20
minutes.

Fruit punch

20 cups (4.5l) (4 quarts) water
2¼ cups (575ml) (1 pint) pineapple juice
3½ cups (800ml) (1½ pints) orange juice
1⅛ cup (250ml) (½ pint) lime juice
10 cups (2.25l) (2 quarts) strong cold tea
Up to 4 cups (800g) sugar

Place the sugar in a pan with half the water,
bring to the boil and boil for one or two
minutes. Cool.

When cool add all the other ingredients.
Serve cold with ice, garnished with orange or
lime slices and a few sprigs of mint.

Pineapple water ice

1 large pineapple, cut in half lengthwise
¾ cup (175g) granulated sugar
2 cups (450ml) (¾ pint) water
1 egg white

Heat the sugar and water gently until the sugar is dissolved, then boil for 5 minutes. Cool.

Remove the core from the pineapple and scrape out the flesh with the juice. Blend on maximum speed for 30 seconds. Leave the shells in the fridge to chill.

Add the pineapple pulp to the cold sugar and water syrup and pour into a rigid freezerproof container. Cover, seal and freeze for 3 hours until half-frozen.

Whisk the egg white until stiff, then gradually whisk in the pineapple ice until frothy. Cover, seal and freeze until firm. Transfer from the freezer to the fridge ten minutes before serving in the chilled pineapple shells.

Golden peach pie

Pastry for a 20cm (9″) double crust pie
4 – 5 cups (approx 800g) canned sliced peaches
½ cup (100g) sugar
2 tablespoons flour
¼ teaspoon ground nutmeg
2 tablespoons butter or margarine
1 tablespoon lemon juice
½ teaspoon grated orange peel
A few drops almond essence

Preheat the oven to 400°F, 200°C, Gas Mark 6.

Drain the peaches, reserving ⅓ cup (75ml) of the syrup.

In a heavy-based pan combine the sugar, flour, nutmeg and a pinch of salt with the reserved syrup. Cook over a medium heat, stirring constantly, until thick and bubbling.

Cool for several minutes, then add the butter, lemon juice, peel and almond extract, followed by the peaches.

Line a 20cm (9″) pie dish with pastry and fill with the peach mixture. Place a pastry lid on the pie, cutting slits to allow steam to escape.

Bake for about 40 minutes until golden brown.

This pie is delicious eaten warm or cold.

Caribbean Johnny or Journey cakes

1½ cups (300g) plain flour
Just under ¼ cup (40g) lard
¼ cup (50g) margarine
2 – 3 tablespoons grated coconut
½ cup (115ml) (¼ pint) coconut milk
2 teaspoons baking powder
¼ teaspoon salt

Preheat the oven to 280°C, 450°F, Gas Mark 8. Grease a large baking tray.

Sift the flour, baking powder and salt.

Melt the margarine over a low heat and add this slowly to the flour, mixing well.

Add the coconut and stir in the milk gradually.

Roll spoonsful of the mixture into small balls and flatten with a fork. Bake for 20 minutes until firm and golden.

Slice and butter the cakes when they are still warm.

They are delicious eaten warm, but also very good for a journey!

Rice salad

2 cups cooked brown rice
2 – 3 chopped spring onions
1 cup (150g) finely chopped celery pieces
½ cup (50g) raisins or sultanas
½ cup (50g) split peanuts
½ cup (50g) toasted cashew pieces
2 tablespoons sesame seeds
1 cup (150g) mixed red and green pepper slices
Fresh chopped parsley or coriander if wished.

For the dressing:

3 tablespoons sesame oil
½ cup (115ml) orange juice
1 clove garlic, crushed
2 tablespoons soy sauce
1 teaspoon salt
1 – 2 tablespoons honey or brown sugar
2 tablespoons cider, apple or wine vinegar
1 cup (200g) finely chopped pineapple — fresh or canned

Mix all the indredients for the dressing in a large bowl, then add the cooked rice. Mix well together and add the dried fruit, nuts and vegetables. Garnish with parsley or coriander.

Coconut kisses

3 egg whites
½ teaspoon vanilla essence
1 cup (200g) granulated sugar
4 cups (400g) cornflakes
1 cup (150g) flaked coconut
1 cup (100g) chopped nuts
¼ cup (50g) dark chocolate
2 teaspoons butter

Preheat the oven to 350°F, 180°C, Gas Mark 4 and grease two baking trays.

Beat the egg whites with a pinch of salt and the vanilla essence until they form soft peaks. Gradually beat in the sugar, then stir in the cereal, coconut and nuts.

Drop in spoonsful onto the baking trays and bake for 18 – 20 minutes.

Remove the cookies onto a wire rack immediately.

When they are cold, melt the chocolate and the butter together and drizzle over the cookies.

Coconut macaroons

2 egg whites
½ teaspoon vanilla essence
⅔ cup (140g) granulated sugar
1 cup (150g) flaked coconut

Preheat the oven to 325°F, 170°C, Gas Mark 3 and grease two baking trays.

Beat the egg whites with the vanilla essence and a pinch of salt until they form soft peaks. Gradually add the sugar, beating until stiff, then fold in the coconut.

Drop in spoonsful onto the greased baking sheets and bake in a slow oven for about 20 minutes.

Leave to cool in the trays for several minutes before removing onto a wire rack to cool completely.

Chocolate coconut drops

2 cups (400g) sugar
½ cup (100g) cocoa
½ cup (100g) butter
¾ cup (170ml) (³/₈ pint) milk
1 cup (100g) chopped nuts
1 teaspoon vanilla essence
3 cups (600g) quick porridge oats
1 cup (100g) desiccated coconut

Mix the sugar and cocoa together in a pan, add the milk and the butter cut into small pieces. Bring to the boil slowly and then boil for 5 minutes.

Remove from the heat and add the vanilla essence. Cool the mixture slightly before adding the oats, coconut and nuts.

Drop teaspoonsful onto a baking tray covered with waxed paper and leave to harden.

Mango-papaya jam

8 cups (1.5 kilos) peeled mango slices
8 cups (1.5 kilos) papaya slices
5 cups (1 litre) (2 pints) water
8 cups (1.5 kilos) sugar

Cook the mango slices in 2½ cups (500ml) (1 pint) water until tender. Press through a coarse sieve.

Cook the papaya in the remaining water until soft.

Combine the mango and papaya, add the sugar and cook slowly for about an hour until the mixture becomes quite thick.

Pour into hot sterilised jars and seal.

Mixed fruit jam

1 cup (200g) finely cut banana
1 cup (200g) finely chopped mango
1 cup (00g) finely chopped pineapple
2⅓ cups (470g) sugar
¾ cup (170ml) (³/₈ pint) water
Cinnamon stick

Cook fruit in the water with the sugar and cinnamon, stirring well. Bring it to the boil then reduce the heat and simmer until very thick.

Pour into warm sterilised jars and seal.

Rose petal and rhubarb jam

2 cups (400g) cut and prepared rhubarb
Juice of 1 small lemon
2 cups (400g) sugar
½ cup (100g) dark red rose petals

Place the rhubarb in a large bowl with the lemon juice and sugar and leave overnight.

The following morning cut freshly picked dry rose petals into small pieces and add to the mixture.

In a heavy based pan boil the mixture until it is thick and at setting point.

Pour into warm sterilised jars and seal.

IV
AUTUMN

VI

AUTUMN

1. SPIDER LORE

Autumn poem

Here Madam Spider spins and weaves
Her web under the low eaves,
Plotting to take and hold in share
The wing'd unwary passenger.
A dragonfly and bee, in dire suspense,
Hang there for evidence…

Fan Ch'eng-ta, "Autumn Poems" *Anthology of Chinese Literature*, ed. C. Birch & D. Keene, Penguin, 1967.

Wilbur's boast

A spider's web is stronger than it looks. Although it is made of thin, delicate strands, the web is not easily broken. However, a web gets torn every day by the insects that kick around in it, and a spider must rebuild it when it gets full of holes. Charlotte liked to do her weaving during the late afternoon, and Fern liked to sit nearby and watch. One afternoon she heard a most interesting conversation and witnessed a strange event.

"You have awfully hairy legs, Charlotte," said Wilbur, as the spider busily worked at her task.

"My legs are hairy for a good reason," replied Charlotte. "Furthermore, each leg of mine has seven sections — the coxa, the trochanter, the femur, the patella, the tibia, the metatarsus, and the tarsus."

Wilbur sat bolt upright. "You're kidding," he said.

"No, I'm not, either."

"Say those names again, I didn't catch them the first time."

"Coxa, trochanter, femur, patella, tibia, metatarus, and tarsus."

"Goodness!" said Wilbur, looking down at his own chubby legs. "I don't think my legs have seven sections."

"Well," said Charlotte, "you and I lead different lives. You don't have to spin a web. That takes real leg work."

"I could spin a web if I tried," said Wilbur, boasting. "I've just never tried."

"Let's see you do it," said Charlotte. Fern chuckled softly, and her eyes grew wide with love for the pig.

"O.K.," replied Wilbur. "You coach me and I'll spin one. It must be a lot of fun to spin a web. How do I start?"

"Take a deep breath!" said Charlotte, smiling. Wilbur breathed deeply. "Now climb to the highest place you can get to, like this." Charlotte raced up to the top of the doorway. Wilbur scrambled to the top of the manure pile.

"Very good!" said Charlotte. "Now make an attachment with your spinnerets, hurl yourself into space, and let out a dragline as you go down!"

Wilbur hesitated a moment, then jumped out into the air. He glanced hastily behind to see if a piece of rope was following him to check his fall, but nothing seemed to be happening in his rear, and the next thing he knew he landed with a thump. "Oooomp!" he grunted.

Charlotte laughed so hard her web began to sway.

"What did I do wrong?" asked the pig, when he recovered from his bump.

"Nothing," said Charlotte. "It was a nice try."

From *Charlotte's Web* by E. B. White.

2. NANCY STORIES

From Ananse to Anancy

Children the world over and from time immemorial always have been so good at inventing stories to wriggle out of trouble. In such instances many a Caribbean adult might be heard to say "Chile, don't come to me with no Nancy story, you hear." Nancy stories have now come to include all manner of tall and outlandish tales, but this wasn't always so. As Louise Benett, the undisputed queen of Jamaican Folklore would probably sum it up "Is Anancy mek it."

This Anancy or Anansi has his origins in West Africa and is known to the Akan people as Ananse, meaning spider. This mythical, magical folk hero who is both man and spider was said to be admired by the gods themselves

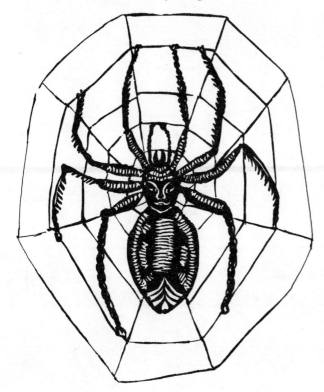

for his wit and initiative. According to the West African folk tales, Ananse not only brought the stories from the gods, he also brought the sun, moon and stars into the world.

With the arrival of European explorers in the Caribbean and the Americas in the 16th century, there followed the enslavement of peoples taken from the West Coast of Africa and used as cheap labour on sugar and cotton plantations in the Caribbean and the Southern States of North America. Naturally the African peoples preserved as much of their oral traditions as they could and though serious attempts were made to suppress their languages and culture, their stories survived particularly in the guise of their folk hero Brer Anancy, in the Caribbean, Brer Rabbit in America. Strangely enough in Dominic he has survived as Compère Lapin, Godfather Rabbit along with other local characters such as Savant-passé-personne (Wiser-than-anyone), Mauvais-passé-diable (Worse-than-the-devil), Rwa-connet-tout (The-king-who-knows-everything).

In the Caribbean the Akan god Nyame is replaced by Tiger as the all-powerful ruler against whom Anancy must now pit his wits in order to obtain the stories and he does.

If Anancy is more cunning, greedy and lazy, perhaps altogether more ruthless than the African Ananse, it is perhaps because life under enslavement for the African peoples in the Caribbean was far more brutal than anything they had experienced in Africa. That is perhaps why as a symbol of the weak's revolt against the powerful oppressor, Anancy has remained as popular and as alive as ever, the inspiration for countless songs, poems, stories, theses, arguments, discussions, debates and he will no doubt continue to be a folk hero for a long time to come.

ANANCY THE SPIDERMAN

1. A-nan-cy is a spi-der, A-nan-cy is a man, A-nan-cy is West In-dian

an West Af-ri-can. A-nan-cy sailed to Eng-lan on a ba-na-na boat, An

when he got to Brix-ton, ev'-ry-bo-dy gave a shout. **Chorus** A-nan-cy! _____ A-

-nan-cy! _____ A-nan-cy_ the mag-ic spi-der-man. A-

-nan-cy! _____ A-nan-cy! _____ A-nan-cy_ an Brer Eng-lish-man.

2. Anancy is a jiver, he's frisky as a fly.
   A shifty plastic being, an that is no lie.
   Anancy is a trickster, he's sensitive to guile,
   He sometimes can be like a very greedy chile.
   Chorus...

These rhythms can be used:

Guitar

Bongos or congas

Maracas

Words by Manley Young.
Music by Chris Cameron.

An African Ananse story

Long, long ago when all the stories of the world belonged to the Akan god Nyame, the god-of-all-things, Ananse the Spider-Man decided that he wanted to buy the stories. So he spun a web up to the sky and asked Nyame for the stories. The sky god was amused. "Ah, but can you pay my price Ananse?" he chuckled. "What is your price, Nyame?" asked Ananse.

"If you want my stories," went on Nyame stroking the golden box next to his royal stool in which the stories were kept, "you must bring me three things. Firstly you must bring me Osebo, the leopard-of-the-terrible-teeth. Secondly, Minboro the hornets-who-sting-like-fire and thirdly, Minoatia the fairy-who-is-never-seen. Bring me those three things" laughed Nyame, "and my stories shall be yours, Ananse." Ananse bowed to the god-of-all-things, spun a web back to earth and set to work. First he went in search of Osebo, the leopard-of-the-terrible-teeth. He went into the part of the jungle where he knew Osebo was likely to be prowling. Osebo saw Ananse coming and licked his lips. "How did you know it was my dinner time Ananse?" he asked. Ananse replied very calmly "Before you eat me Osebo, can we play the binding game?" "What's that?" asked Osebo who liked playing games when he wasn't hungry. "It's a game you play with vine creepers," explained Ananse. "First, I will bind you by the foot like this, then I will untie you and you can bind me."

"Oh alright," growled Osebo who intended to eat Ananse when it was his turn to bind him. Ananse bound Osebo very tightly by the feet and hung him on the branch of a tree. "Now you are ready to meet the god-of-all-things," he said.

Next he went to catch Minboro, the hornets-who-sting-like-fire. First he filled a calabash with water. Then he cut a huge leaf from a banana tree. Creeping through the grass up close to Minboro's nest, he held the banana leaf over his head like an umbrella and poured some of the water from the calabash over his head. The rest he emptied over the hornets' nest and called out "It is raining, raining, raining. Why don't you fly into my calabash and shelter from the rain."

The hornets, who hated getting their delicate wings wet and tattered, accepted gratefully and flew one by one into the calabash. "You too, Minboro, are ready to meet Nyame the god-of-all-things," Ananse said, quickly covering the hole in the calabash and hanging it on the tree next to Osebo.

Ananse's last task was to catch Minoatia, the fairy-who-is-never-seen. First he carved a little wooden doll holding a bowl which he filled with crushed buttered yams. He covered the doll with sticky latex gum and placed it under a flamboyant tree where he knew fairies liked to dance. He tied one end of a vine round the doll's head and holding the other end in his hand he hid behind a bush.

Soon Minoatia, the fairy-who-is-never-seen came dancing, dancing under the flamboyant tree. She saw the wooden doll with the bowl of yams. Minoatia suddenly felt very hungry. "Gum baby," she said, "May I eat some of your yams?" From his hiding place, Ananse pulled at the vine so that the doll seemed to nod its head. "Thank you, gum baby," said Minoatia, and taking the bowl, she ate every bit of the yams. When she had finished eating she thanked the doll again but this time she got no response. "I said, 'Thank you'," repeated the fairy but she still got no reply.

"Don't you answer when I talk to you?" she said crossly. "You are very rude, gum baby, and need to be taught a lesson. Take that!" She slapped the doll with her right hand and stuck

fast. "Let go of me, gum baby, or you'll get another one." she said angrily. She slapped the doll with the other hand and that too stuck fast. Minoatia kicked and wriggled until she was stuck so firmly she could no longer move an inch.

Ananse came up quickly and took her to the tree where the leopard and hornets were waiting, saying, "Minoatia you are going to meet Nyame, the god-of-all-things."

Ananse tied a net round his captives, spun a web up to the sky and pulling them up behind him he lay them at Nyame's feet.

"Here is the price of your stories, oh Nyame." he said, bowing humbly. "Please accept Osebo, the leopard-of-the-terrible-teeth, Minboro, the hornets-who-sting-like-fire and Minoatia, the fairy-who-is-never-seen."

Even Nyame, the god-of-all-things was greatly impressed. He called to his nobles to gather round. "Little Ananse has brought me the price of my stories. Let everyone sing his praises. From now on all my stories shall belong to him."

True to his word, Nyame gave his golden box of stories over to Ananse the Spider Man who spun another web and went back to his village and his people clutching his precious box of stories. You could call it fate or was it perhaps Nyame having a last laugh? Whatever it was, on arriving in his village the box flew open and all the stories scattered to every corner of the earth, including this one.

This tale has been told in a thousand ways: Please tell it again till the end of your days!

Jane Grell.

Activities around Anancy

Read as many Anancy stories as you can. Spot any differences between the tales from Africa and those from the Caribbean.

Create your very own version of Anancy the Spider Man, complete with web. He could be a wall frieze or hang like a mobile from the ceiling. Use any combination of materials from fabric, pipe-cleaners, wool, wood, card, glue, felt pens, etc. Compare your illustration of Anancy with those of other artists.

From Anancy stories to personal stories

Using a cardboard box and gold paper or fabric make a golden box. Invite the children or party guests to bring an object of personal interest or value. Put the objects in the box to represent some of the stories which flew from Anancy's box. Get each owner to tell the story behind their object.

It will prove so clearly the facts that:
Everyone can tell a story;
Everyone has a story to tell.

---

3. HARVEST

Manu's sons

... May she, the Queen of all that is and is to be, may Earth make ample space and room for us.

Not so over-crowded by the crowd of Manu's sons, she who hath many heights and floods and level plains;

She who bears plants endowed with many varied powers, may Earth for us spread wide and favour us.

In whom the sea, and the great river, and the waters, in whom our food and cornlands had their being...

From "Atharua Veda XII", *The Hindu Tradition*, ed. A. Embree, Random House 1966.

Harvest memory

When they had arrived at the first harvest-field, the men would line up at the edge, naked to the loins, their sickles at the ready. Then my Uncle Lansana or some other farmer — for the harvest

threw people together and everyone lent a hand in each other's harvesting — would invite them to begin work. At once the black torsos would bend over the great golden field, and the sickles would begin the reaping. Now it was not only the breeze of morning that was making the whole field sway and shiver, but the men also, with their sickles.

These sickles kept rising and falling with astonishing rapidity and regularity. They had to cut the stalk between the bottom joint and the lowest leaf, so that only the leaf was left behind; well, they hardly ever missed. Of course, such a degree of accuracy depended on the reaper: he would hold the ear with one hand and incline the stalk to receive a clean blow from the sickle. He would reap the ears one by one, but the swift rise and fall of the sickle was nevertheless amazing. Besides, each man made it a point of honour to reap as accurately and as swiftly as possible; he would move forward across the field with a bunch of stalks in his hand, and his fellow-workmen would judge his skill by the number and size of his sheaves.

Camara Laye, *The African Child*.

SONG OF THE HARVEST HOE

Traditional   Chinese work song

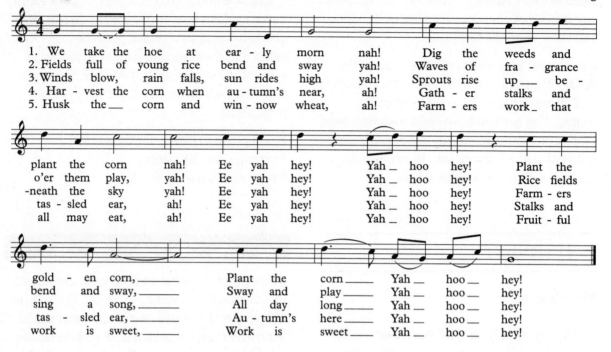

1. We take the hoe at ear-ly morn nah! Dig the weeds and plant the corn nah! Ee yah hey! Yah __ hoo hey! Plant the gold-en corn, _____ Plant the corn _____ Yah __ hoo __ hey!
2. Fields full of young rice bend and sway yah! Waves of fra-grance o'er them play, yah! Ee yah hey! Yah __ hoo hey! Rice fields bend and sway, _____ Sway and play _____ Yah __ hoo __ hey!
3. Winds blow, rain falls, sun rides high yah! Sprouts rise up __ be- -neath the sky yah! Ee yah hey! Yah __ hoo hey! Farm-ers sing a song, _____ All day long _____ Yah __ hoo __ hey!
4. Har-vest the corn when au-tumn's near, ah! Gath-er stalks and tas-sled ear, ah! Ee yah hey! Yah __ hoo hey! Stalks and tas-sled ear, _____ Au-tumn's here _____ Yah __ hoo __ hey!
5. Husk the __ corn and win-now wheat, ah! Farm-ers work __ that all may eat, ah! Ee yah hey! Yah __ hoo hey! Fruit-ful work is sweet, _____ Work is sweet _____ Yah __ hoo __ hey!

The Boggart (or clever reaping)

English folk tale from Lincolnshire, a large county on the eastern side of England. Much of the land is very fertile and farming has always been very important there. Many tales are told about the clever ways of the Lincolnshire farmers. This story is a particular favourite.

There was once a Lincolnshire farmer who was on the look out for a bit more land to add to his farm. He was very pleased when his neighbour sold him a patch where the soil was rich and good and the land was flat.

The day after the sale the farmer went to look at the land to decide what crop he would put there first. He had scarcely got there when a Boggart appeared from nowhere, a fearsomely hairy creature waving his long arms around and jumping up and down on his short thick legs.

"Clear off!" he said to the farmer. "You're on my land!"

"Clear off yourself!" replied the farmer, "I've just bought it."

"It's mine! It's mine! It's mine!" yelled the Boggart, waving his arms more than ever, stamping his huge feet and shaking his ugly head.

The farmer didn't want to argue with such a creature, but nor did he want to give up any of the land. "I don't want to take from you something that's yours," he said, "but I don't want you to take anything from me that's rightly mine either. So let's strike a bargain."

The Boggart grinned a wide hairy grin: "Agreed!" he said. "You do the work and we'll share the crops!"

"Fine!" replied the farmer. "When I've grown the crops, what do you want, Tops or Bottoms?"

"Tops!" said the Boggart, thinking he had got the better of the farmer.

The clever farmer sowed potatoes on the land. At harvest time, when the Boggart came to collect his share, he had only the shrivelled leaves while the farmer had several tons of fine potatoes. But there was nothing the Boggart could do, the farmer had kept to his part of the bargain. However, when the farmer asked the Boggart what he would have the following year the Boggart, determined not to be tricked again, said "Bottoms!"

So the farmer planted barley. When the crop was ready the farmer cut it and stored it away in one of his barns and the Boggart was left with nothing except the old roots and stubble of the barley. He was furious! But a bargain is a bargain, so he couldn't complain. But he had a clever idea about the next crop:

"This year you'll sow wheat," he said. "When it's ready for harvest we'll each mow it and keep what we mow." Boggart knew that he

was much stronger than the farmer, and reckoned that he could mow much faster and collect most of the crop. The farmer was very worried, but a wise friend in the village suggested a plan. So the farmer went to the village blacksmith and asked him to make some iron rods. He took them to the wheatfield and scattered them in the corn on the side the Boggart was going to mow.

On the day of the harvest it was hot and dry. The Boggart arrived, scythe over his shoulder, grinning from hairy ear to ear. The farmer and he started to mow from opposite ends of the land. The farmer moved steadily, but the Boggart kept striking the iron rods and blunting his scythe. He thought the rods were weeds, because he knew no better.

By midday the farmer had mowed half the field and the Boggart had only managed a small corner. As the sun blazed down the Boggart got crosser and crosser. At last, after stopping for the thirtieth time, the Boggart gave up. He flung down his blunt scythe and screamed, "Keep the useless land. I'll have nothing more to do with it!" He jumped into the air and came down so hard that a hole opened up in the ground and he vanished into it. The Boggart never bothered the farmer again, but sometimes, when it is nearly harvest time, tools go missing from farms in the area. People are sure it is the Boggart at work!

Lentil and vegetable stew

Enjoy the Boggart story with hot harvest supper:

1 cup (200g) brown lentils
2 potatoes, diced
3 courgettes or 1 small marrow, sliced
2 leeks, trimmed and sliced
1 stalk celery, sliced
Juice of 1 lemon
1 onion, chopped
2 cloves garlic, crushed
Salt and pepper
Oil
2 tablespoons finely chopped parsley

Soak the lentils overnight. Drain them and then simmer in 2 cups (450ml) (1 pint) water until nearly soft. Add the potatoes, courgettes, leeks and celery, season with salt and pepper and cook, with a close fitting lid on the pan, until the vegetables are tender. Fry the onion until soft and brown and add the garlic. Combine the onion and garlic with the other vegetables, and add the lemon juice and the parsley.

Simmer for a few minutes longer and serve with rice or wholemeal bread.

4. KITE FLYING FESTIVAL

Autumn kite flying (September)

There are distinctive eastern and western traditions of kite flying as a festive autumn event. In the British Isles, kites are flown to celebrate Michaelmas, The Feast of St Michael which coincides with traditional harvest fare. Known as Michael the Victorious or Michael nam Buadh, this patron saint is held as a conqueror of evil. Legends portray him as slaying a dragon, and folk plays enact this in timeless fashion using the figure of St George to carry out the symbolic deed. Kites are flown possibly to reach literally away from earth and 'towards heaven', possibly because you must wrestle with the wind to fly a kite well, or quite simply because it is great fun.

The Chinese dragon represents forces more of life and creativity and is a positive figure. The Chinese Double Ninth Festival falls on the ninth day of the ninth lunar month and recalls a story going back to the Han Dynasty of ancient times. A wise clairvoyant warned that a great disaster would occur, but only one person would heed his warning. This man — whom some called Woon Ging, tried to warn others too but none would listen. Woon Ging led his family to a high mountain top, wearing tiny pieces of dogwood to ward off evil and taking kites with which to reach up on the winds towards the heavens. They were the only survivors of a natural disaster; whether it was floods or earthquake defies memory now. So it represents good fortune and good luck to climb to a high place on the Double Ninth and fly kites.

Enormous skill and artistry can be put into making the kites. Some hold tiny chimes or bells to make noises in the wind. Some are complicated piece patterns, such as animals with moving body parts.

Why not set aside a special day for kite flying? Even better, plan ahead and enjoy constructing your kite first!

Dragon — a good group project!

You need:

At least 12 sticks about 60cm (24") long
Weaving cane
Paper and glue
String and curtain ring
Coloured streamers
Paints or crayons

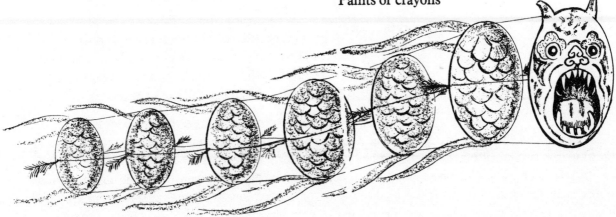

This is a difficult kite to make and an even more difficult one to fly. But the results can be really spectacular.

The Dragon kite is made of several kites joined together. The longer the Dragon, the more difficult it is to manage, so try one with only six or seven sections to begin with.

1. To make one section, mark the centre of two of the sticks and bind and glue them together into a cross. Soak the cane in water for half an hour. Bend a piece of cane into a circle round the cross. Let the ends overlap and bind and glue them together. Bind the cane to the sticks where it touches them. Cover the frame with paper.

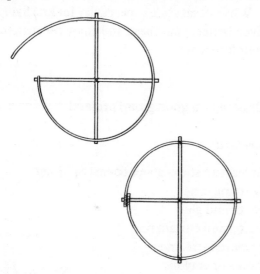

2. Make at least five more sections in the same way, each one a little smaller than the one before.

3. Make 12 large paper tassels and glue one to each side of each of the kite's sections.

4. Cut four pieces of string 30cm (12″) long. Use them to join two kite sections together, one behind the other. You will have to make tiny holes in the covers so that you can thread the string through them and tie the ends firmly to the sticks. Make sure you tie the top of one section to the top of the second one, the right side of one section to the right side of the next one, and so on.

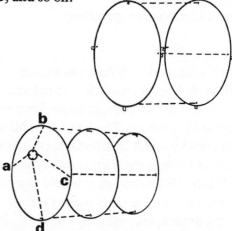

5. Join all six or seven sections one behind the other in the same way, the largest section at the front and the smallest one at the back.

Bridles:

Cut two pieces of string long enough to reach from 'a' to 'b' to 'c'. Tie the ends of one of the pieces to points 'a' and 'c', remembering to loop it through the curtain ring. Tie the ends of the second piece to points 'b' and 'd'. The ring should be about one third of the way along the second bridle.

Decoration:

Paint the dragon's fiery eyes and gaping jaws on the front section of the kite and paint scales on all the others. Attach coloured streamers all round the edge of all the sections.

If you prefer, you can make the dragon of square or hexagonal sections instead of circles, as long as they are all made in exactly the same way and spaced exactly the same distance apart. The sections should graduate down in size, with the largest one at the front.

5. THANKSGIVING

American Thanksgiving

The American festival of Thanksgiving was first celebrated in November 1621 in the tiny colony of Plymouth, Massachusetts. A small group of protestant dissenters, the Pilgrims, had arrived in December 1620 seeking to build a new life of religious freedom in the New World. Their tiny ship, the Mayflower, en route for the colony of Jamestown in Virginia, was blown off course by gales and landed in mid-winter on the cold and inhospitable shore of what is now Massachusetts. The Pilgrims survived that first winter through the help of the Native American people who befriended them, and showed them which of the unknown plants were good to eat. After the successful harvest the following year, the English settlers held a feast to give thanks for the harvested food which would see them through the coming winter, for their survival during their first terrible months, for their safe arrival in the new land of religious freedom, and for the friendship of the native peoples who had helped them. At the first Thanksgiving feast the Pilgrims ate the foods which the Native Americans had shown them: turkey, pumpkins, corn, sweet potatoes and cranberries. Legends say that the native people also showed the Pilgrims how to bury a fish with the corn seed when planting in the spring to fertilize the soil, and also how to make popcorn!

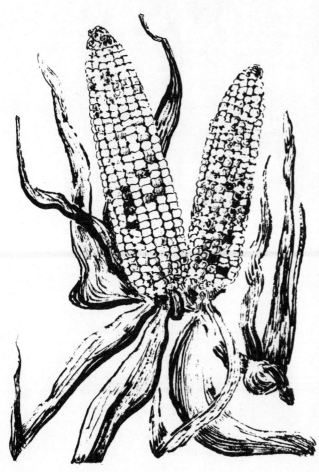

Thanksgiving is more than a harvest festival, although harvest is one of its main themes. It is also about a new beginning in a new homeland. The symbolic foods give a picture of new sources of nourishment, brought through a relationship with new people.

My own family, like the families of many other Americans, is of mixed heritage. My father's ancestors arrived from England as early as 1643. My mother's family were Russian and Polish Jews. Our family celebration of Thanksgiving was linked to gratitude for their safe arrival in America and for the freedom of religious expression. My mother always cooked the traditional Thanksgiving foods according to Polish-Jewish recipes, as her mother and grandmothers had done. And like them, our table always included strangers and outsiders, people who had no home or family of their own. For this festival is surely about friendship, family, and hope!

Jenni Lauruol.

IROQUOIS LULLABY

Traditional

Unaccompanied

Ho   ho _____ wa - ta - nay,   Ho,   ho _____ wa - ta - nay,
Sleep   sleep _____ lit - tle one,   Sleep,   sleep _____ lit - tle one,

Ho   ho _____ wa - ta - nay, Ki   yo - ke - na, Ki   yo - ke - na.
Sleep   sleep _____ lit - tle one, Oh   go   to   sleep, Oh   go   to   sleep.

CANOE ROUND

My paddle's keen and bright / flashing like silver,
Follow the wild goose flight / dip, dip and swing.

Dip, dip and swing her back / flashing like silver,
Follow the wild goose track / dip, dip and swing.

Margaret Embers McGee, 1918

Treats from corn

The first settlers in America had never known of eating corn. They learned lots of ways of using it from the native Indians. Sometimes they would use molasses to make delicious sweet treats with corn.

When making your own sweets remember that they often have to be cooked at high temperatures, so make sure there is an adult nearby to help you. It is also worth remembering that the best sweets are made on warm dry days: if the weather is damp or sticky you can be fairly sure that everything else is going to end up sticky too!

Crackerjack:

2 cups of sugar
1 cup of molasses or ½ cup of black treacle
2 tablespoons of vinegar
½ teaspoon of bicarbonate of soda
About 8 cups of mixed popped corn and peanuts

Put the molasses, sugar and vinegar into a large pan and boil for about five minutes.

Have a small saucer of cold water ready and drop a tiny spoonful of the mixture into the water. If the mixture cracks, it is ready. It can take anything from five to twenty minutes for the mixture to reach this cracking point, depending on your pan and your cooker.

When the mixture is at cracking point, take it off the heat and add the bicarbonate of soda, stirring well with a wooden spoon. Then stir in the popped corn and peanuts.

Line a baking tray with waxed paper and pour the mixture into the tray to set. Try and cut it into pieces before it is completely set.

Popcorn balls:

1 cup molasses — or ½ cup black treacle
1 cup sugar
1 tablespoon butter
About 8 cups of popped corn

Put the molasses, sugar and butter into a large pan and bring to the boil, stirring gently. Leave to boil for about ten minutes.

Have a small saucer of cold water ready and drop a tiny spoonful of the mixture into the water. If it forms a firm ball, it is ready. This is known as the 'hard ball' stage. It can take anything from ten minutes up to half an hour to reach this hard ball stage.

When the mixture is at this stage, take it off the heat and add the popcorn, stirring thoroughly to coat all the corn. Leave to cool for at least five minutes.

Then grease your hands lightly with cooking oil or butter and roll handfuls of the mixture into balls. Put these balls onto waxed paper to harden.

Corn chips

1 cup (200g) yellow cornmeal
²/₃ cup (140g) flour
1 teaspoon salt
1 teaspoon baking powder
2 tablespoons dried milk powder
½ cup (115ml) (¼ pint) water
¼ cup (55ml) (¹/₈ pint) oil
½ teaspoon Worcestershire sauce
2 or 3 drops Tabasco sauce

Preheat the oven to 350°F, 180°C, Gas mark 4.
Grease two baking trays and sprinkle each with
cornmeal.

Mix all the dry ingredients together in a large
bowl and add all the liquid ingredients. Stir
everything together with a fork. Knead for a
few minutes until the mixutre is smooth.

Divide the dough in half and roll out each half
as thin as you can directly onto the baking trays,
using a floured rolling pin. Sprinkle lightly with
paprika or seasoned salt and run the rolling pin
over the rolled dough once more.

Prick all over with a fork and cut into squares or
triangles.

Bake for 10 minutes, or until the chips are
lightly browned.

Pumpkin pie

3 cups (675ml) pumpkin purée
¾ cup (170ml) honey
2 tablespoons molasses
¼ teaspoon powdered cloves
3 teaspoons cinnamon
1½ teaspoons ground ginger
1 teaspoon salt
4 eggs, lightly beaten
1 large can evaporated milk or 2 cups (450ml)
    scalded milk

Preheat the oven to 450°F, 230°C, Gas Mark 8.
Have ready a 22cm (9″) wholewheat pie shell.

Mix all the ingredients together in the order
given in the list above. Pour into the pie shell
and bake for 10 minutes in the hot oven, then
reduce the temperature to 350°F, 180°C, Gas
Mark 4 and bake for a further 40 minutes or
until set.

For a delicious pumpkin pudding leave out the
pie shell! Butter a baking dish and pour in the
pumpkin mixture. Bake in the same way as the
pie, but serve, still hot, with vanilla ice cream or
thick cream!

A rootabaga story

The Huckabuck family and how they raised popcorn in Nebraska and quit and came back.

Jonas Jonas Huckabuck was a farmer in Nebraska with a wife Mama Mama Huckabuck, and a daughter, Pony Pony Huckabuck.

"Your father gave you two names the same in front," people had said to him.

And he answered, "Yes, two names are easier to remember. If you call me by my first name Jonas and I don't hear you then when you call me by my second name Jonas maybe I will."

"And," he went on, "I can call my pony-face girl Pony Pony because if she doesn't hear me the first time she always does the second."

And so they lived on a farm where they raised popcorn, these three, Jonas Jonas Huckabuck, his wife, Mama Mama Huckabuck, and their pony-faced daughter, Pony Pony Huckabuck.

After they harvested the crop one year they had the barns, the cribs, the sheds, the shacks, and all the cracks and corners of the farm, all filled with popcorn.

"We came out to Nebraska to raise popcorn," said Jonas Jonas. "And I guess we got nearly enough popcorn this year for the popcorn poppers and all the friends and relations of all the popcorn poppers in these United States."

And this was the year Pony Pony was going to bake her first squash pie all by herself. In one corner of the corn crib, all covered over with popcorn, she had a secret, a big round squash, a fat yellow squash, a rich squash all spotted with spots of gold.

And there was a shine of silver. And Pony Pony wondered why silver should be in a squash. She picked and plunged with her fingers till she pulled it out.

"It's a buckle," she said. "A silver buckle, a Chinese silver slipper buckle."

She ran with it to her father and said, "Look what I found when I cut open the golden yellow squash spotted with gold spots — it is a Chinese silver slipper buckle."

"It means our luck is going to change, and we don't know whether it will be good luck or bad luck," said Jonas Jonas to his daughter Pony Pony Huckabuck.

Then she ran with it to her mother and said, "Look what I found when I cut open the yellow squash spotted with spots of gold — it is a Chinese silver slipper buckle."

"It means our luck is going to change, and we don't know whether it will be good luck or bad luck," said Mama Mama Huckabuck.

And that night a fire started in the barns, cribs, sheds, shacks, cracks and corners where the popcorn harvest was kept. All night long the popcorn popped. In the morning the ground, all the farmhouse and the barn were covered with white popcorn, so it looked like a heavy fall of snow.

All the next day the fire kept on and the popcorn popped till it was up to the shoulders of Pony Pony when she tried to walk from the house to the barn. And that night in all the barns, cribs, sheds, shacks, cracks, and corners of the farm, the popcorn went on popping.

In the morning when Jonas Jonas Huckabuck looked out of the upstairs window he saw the popcorn popping and coming higher and higher. It was nearly up to the window. Before evening and dark of that day, Jonas Jonas Huckabuck, and his wife Mama Mama Huckabuck, and their daughter Pony Pony Huckabuck, all went away from the farm saying, "We came to Nebraska to raise popcorn but this is too much. We will not come back till the wind blows away the popcorn. We will not come back till we get a sign and a signal."

They went to Oskaloosa, Iowa. And the next year Pony Pony Huckabuck was very proud because when she stood on the sidewalks in the street she could see her father sitting high on the seat of a coal wagon, driving two big spanking horses hitched with shining brass harness in front of the coal wagon. And though Pony Pony and Jonas Jonas were proud, very proud all that year, there never came a sign, a signal.

The next year again was a proud year, exactly as proud a year as they spent in Oskaloosa. They went to Paducah, Kentucky, to Defiance, Ohio; Peoria, Illinois; Indianapolis, Indiana; Walla Walla, Washington. And in all these places Pony Pony Huckabuck saw her father, Jonas Jonas Huckabuck standing in rubber boots deep down in a ditch with a shining steel shovel shoveling yellow clay and black mud from down in the ditch high and high over his shoulders. And though it was a proud year they got no sign, no signal.

The next year came. It was the proudest of all. This was the year Jonas Jonas Huckabuck and his family lived in Elgin, Illinois, and Jonas Jonas was watchman in a watch factory watching the watches.

"I know where you have been," Mama Mama Huckabuck would say of an evening to Pony Pony Huckabuck. "You have been down to the watch factory watching your father watch the watches."

"Yes," said Pony Pony, "yes, and this evening when I was watching father watch the watches in the watch factory, I looked over my left shoulder and I saw a policeman with a star and brass buttons, and he was watching me to see if I was watching father watch the watches in the watch factory."

It was a proud year. Pony Pony saved her money. Thanksgiving came. Pony Pony said, "I am going to get a squash to make a squash pie." She hunted from one grocery to another; she

kept her eyes on the farm wagons coming into Elgin with squashes.

She found what she wanted, the yellow squash spotted with gold spots. She took it home, cut it open, and saw the inside was like the outside, all rich yellow spotted with gold spots.

There was a shine like silver. She picked and plunged with her fingers and pulled and pulled till at last she pulled out the shine of silver.

"It's a sign; it is a signal," she said. "It is a buckle, a slipper buckle, a Chinese silver slipper buckle. It is the mate to the other buckle. Our luck is going to change. Yoo hoo! Yoo hoo!"

She told her father and mother about the buckle. They went back to the farm in

Nebraska. The wind had been blowing and blowing for three years, and all the popcorn was blown away.

"Now we are going to be farmers again," said Jonas Jonas Huckabuck to Mama Mama Huckabuck and to Pony Pony Huckabuck. "And we are going to raise squash, rutabuga, pumpkins, and peppers for pickling. We are going to raise wheat, oats, barley, rye. We are going to raise corn such as Indian corn and kaffir corn — but we are not going to raise popcorn for the popcorn poppers to be popping."

And the pony-faced daughter was proud because she had on new black slippers, and around her ankles holding the slippers on the left foot and the right foot, she had two buckles, silver buckles, Chinese silver slipper buckles. They were mates.

Sometimes on Thanksgiving Day and Christmas and New Year's, she tells her friends to be careful when they open a squash.

"Squashes make your luck change good to bad and bad to good," says Pony Pony.

Carl Sandburg.

6. SUCCOT

Jewish harvest festival

The Jewish harvest festival is celebrated in late September as Succot which culminates in the special day, Simchat Torah. This is a time for giving thanks for food and friendship, for joy and celebration.

The word 'succot' is plural for the Hebrew 'succah' meaning shelter, booth, or tabernacle. For this is a week-long festival which involves making a special shelter for the occasion outside or inside. The roof is made of leafy branches or strands of fabric to remind us to look up through what is above us to the sky and stars and heaven. Fruit and vegetables are hung from the walls as reminders of harvest! If possible — even if the succah is made in the corner of a small room — a table and chairs will be placed inside for prayers, readings, and meals.

Four special articles are needed to observe succot, and there are many meanings for these. First, the etrog fruit, a large lemon-shaped citrus fruit usually imported from Israel.

Secondly, special branches of palm, myrtle and willow. These are bound together to form a 'lulav'. On each day of the festival week (except shabbat or Jewish Sabbath) the lulav and etrog are waved in all directions to show that the goodness of God is all around us. Friends are invited to share in the meals and the blessings.

There are different schools of thought as to possible meanings behind the etrog and lulav. One suggests that the etrog and lulav are like a person:

The palm representing a backbone;

Willow leaves, the mouth;

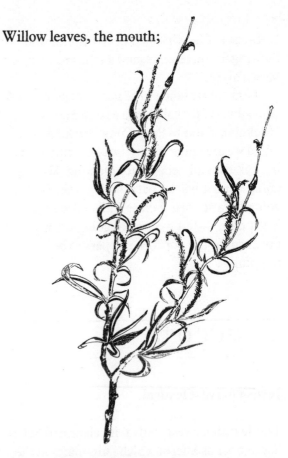

Myrtle leaves, the eyes;

and the etrog, the heart.

In this view the symbols represent our human body as a fruit of creation for which to be thankful, and that worship and thanksgiving should be given by our entire being. Another view says simply that these four plants represent the fruits of the earth and harvest itself.

HINEH MA TOV

Hebrew traditional

1. Hineh ma tov u'mana'yim, shevet achim gam yachad.
   Hineh ma tov u'mana'yim, shevet achim gam yachad.

2. Hineh ma tov, shevet achim gam yachad.
   Hineh ma tov, shevet achim gam yachad.

(Psalm 133. Translation of Hebrew: *Behold how good and pleasant it is for brothers and sisters to live together in unity.*)

SHALOM CHAVERIM

Hebrew traditional

Shalom chaverim / shalom chaverim / shalom / shalom.
Le hit ra-ot / Le hit ra-ot / shalom / shalom.

Glad tidings we bring | of peace on earth | goodwill | toward men.
Of peace on earth | of peace on earth | goodwill | toward men.

Apple candy

8 apples
Water
Sugar
Rosewater

Cut the apples into quarters and core but do not peel them.

Place them in a pan and cover with water. Bring them to the boil then reduce the heat and simmer until very soft. Blend the apples in a blender or put through a sieve.

Use one cup of sugar for each cup of apple pulp. Bring the sugar and pulp to the boil, then lower the heat and simmer for an hour, stirring every few minutes. When the mixture is the consistency of very thick jam, add a tablespoon of rosewater.

Sprinkle a baking tray with caster sugar and pour in the apple mixture. When it is cool, cut into squares and sprinkle with sugar.

Let the candy dry at room temperature for at least a day.

The same process can be followed to make peach or pear candy.

Stuffed cabbage

12 large cabbage leaves
2½ cups (500g) finely minced beef or lamb
¼ cup (50g) rice
2 large onions, finely chopped
1 large carrot, grated
3 tablespoons oil
2 cups (one 400g tin) peeled tomatoes
2 tablespoons sugar
1 teaspoon lemon juice
½ teaspoon salt
Stock

Preheat the oven to 350°F, 180°C, Gas Mark 4.

Wash the cabbage leaves and pour boiling water over them to blanch them. Cut out the hard centre stalks.

Wash the rice, then mix it with the minced meat and half the chopped onion. Put some of this meat mixture onto each cabbage leaf and roll up like a parcel.

Put the oil in a large pan or casserole and fry the rest of the onion with the grated carrot for a few minutes. Add the cabbage rolls to this pan and pour in enough stock to cover them. Add the salt, lemon juice and tomatoes.

Cover the pan or casserole tightly and cook in a moderate oven for about 3 hours.

7. STORIES FOR WHEN THE EVENINGS GROW LONGER

The wise men of Chelm

When the inhabitants of Chelm, who were known for their wisdom, decided to build their city, they began by digging its foundations. Suddenly one of them exclaimed, "Brothers and fellow townsmen! Here we are digging and digging, but what will we do with all the dirt we shovel out?" So the wise men of Chelm thought and decided, "Here is what we will do: we will dig a big hole and dump all the dirt we've shoveled out into it."

"But what will we do with the dirt from the hole?" persisted the questioner.

The wise men of Chelm thought and thought and finally said, "We will dig a second hole in which to dump the dirt from the first one."

Once Chelm had been built and a magnificent synagogue stood in its midst, it was decided to install an alms box. One day the Chelmites came to pray and saw that the box was missing. The rabbi and the wise men of Chelm gave the matter much thought and finally decided to install a new alms box that would hang from the ceiling where thieves could not reach it.

A few days went by, and the beadle came to the rabbi and said, "Rabbi, the alms box is indeed out of reach of the thieves, but it is also out of reach of anyone wishing to give alms." At once the rabbi summoned the wise men of Chelm again, and after a long debate it was resolved to put a ladder in the synagogue to help the alms givers reach the alms box.

And here is something else that happened in Chelm too. One Friday, the rabbi of Chelm bought a fish for his Sabbath meal — and since he was holding his walking stick in one hand and a bag with his prayer shawl and phylacteries in the other, he stuck the fish head down in his jacket pocket with its tail sticking up in the air. As he was walking along, the fish thrashed its tail and struck him in the face. "Did you ever hear of such a thing?" asked the agitated Chelmites. "How dare a fish strike our rabbi!" And so the wise men of Chelm sat in judgement and voted to punish the impudent fish by drowning it in the river.

Ah, the wise men of Chelm! When will we see their like again?

(Note: A 'beadle' was an important person, a religious officer of sorts; 'Phylacteries' are small leather boxes containing Hebrew texts.)

By Hillel Halkin, from *Jewish Folktales*, Collins, 1990.

Manu's ark

There are flood stories in many parts of the world. The Bible story of Noah is probably the best known. The Hindu story of Manu, the first man to live on earth, tells the story of a flood at the very beginning of creation.

Manu, the first man on earth, stood praying in a stream. For years, he had stood on one leg with his arms upstretched to heaven. Nothing, it seemed, could disturb him.

Then one day a little fish nudged his ankle. "Manu! Help! A big fish is trying to eat me!" Even though Manu's mind was on the meaning of life, the universe and the cause of everything, he took pity on the little creature. He scooped it up in a pitcher.

The fish began to grow. It grew and grew so he put it in a tank. It grew and grew, so he heaved it along to the sacred River Ganga. But soon it was squashed between the banks of the holy river. "Take me to the sea," gasped the fish, "or else I'll die!"

Praying to Lord Brahma for strength, Manu hauled it to the ocean. With a wriggle of joy it plunged into the billowing waves.

"Thank you, Manu!" it cried. "You have saved my life! Listen! Lord Brahma, the Creator, is not pleased with this evil world. He wants to destroy everything and start again. Do as I say, and you will be saved."

Manu listened. Then he went out and built a massive boat. He went to every part of the world and collected the seed of every living thing, including the seed of seven holy rishis, the gods and the demons. He carried them all back to the ark, and waited.

The destruction began. Seven blazing suns appeared in the sky, burning fiercely. Wind and fire came like greedy tongues, licking round the world, gobbling everything in their path. Great, black clouds rolled across the sky. With a mighty crack, they split open, and down came the rain.

It rained for twelve years and Lord Brahma destroyed everything except Manu and his ark.

When at last the rain stopped, how lonely Manu felt! The water stretched from one horizon to another. Suddenly he saw a horned fish swimming towards him. Overjoyed, Manu swung a rope over its horns.

Year after year the fish dragged the ark across the never-ending water, until one day, rising out of the misty waves, Manu saw the tip of a mountain. The ark bumped to a standstill on the rocky slopes.

Then the fish spoke. "I am Brahma, Lord of all living things. I saved you from the flood, Manu, so that, when the waters drop, you can create life again."

So Manu set about creating all living things from the seeds on the ark. Soon all the rivers, seas, jungles and deserts were filled with life. The gods were back in their heavens, the demons returned to the underworld. The seven rishis began to pray, and Manu stood on the earth again and thanked God.

Jamila Gavin.

The rabbit and the crocodile
or
How the rabbit nearly wiped out the crocodile nation

With thanks to Kunijwok Kwawang.

A rabbit once married a crocodile.

I should point out that in those days, as all the species of the world lived together in unity and harmony with God, and as they all spoke the same language and were of equal worth in every possible way, there was nothing odd at all in a rabbit marrying a crocodile.

However, at about this time, the dragon-fly displeased God, causing him to abandon the overworld. He took himself off to the underworld, sad that his perfect creation had now been marred, and that the perfect harmony of all living things had been destroyed. From now on, as well as peace, justice and bliss, there would be greed, corruption and great injustice.

Well, back to the rabbit and the crocodiles. There was once a rabbit. Not one of those floppy-eared cuddly rabbits which children like to take to bed with them, but a *rabbit* rabbit, with powerful munching teeth, sharp claws and a cunning brain. His name was Apowojjo. It was Apowojjo's sister who had married a crocodile. An unlikely match you might think, but in those days marriages between the species was still very common, and old habits die hard.

However, it has to be said that for one reason or another, there was bitter rivalry between the two families which extended through all the in-laws and the aunts and uncles and cousins and second cousins and nieces and nephews and on and on.

One day, perhaps out of curiosity, Apowojjo decided to go and visit his sister and see how she was making out with her crocodile husband, Nyang.

His sister, Nyalango, as she was now called, was overjoyed to see her brother. She had been feeling quite cut off. Lovingly, she embraced him and then took him into her home to show off all her numerous babies.

I'm not quite sure what the off-spring of a rabbit and a crocodile look like. Perhaps they had furry bodies instead of reptilian scales; perhaps they had soft round eyes, instead of hard, red ones. At any rate they must have looked soft and tender and delicious, because Apowojjo declared that they were the prettiest things he had ever seen.

Because her brother had arrived unexpectedly, Nyalango wanted to go and collect more firewood for her cooking pot as she would make extra food. Her husband Nyang would be returning home and she wanted everything to be ready.

"Please, brother, would you babysit for me, while I just nip into the forest and collect some more wood? You could stir my broth from time to time, which is hanging there over the fire."

Apowojjo agreed with good grace but, in truth, he wasn't too partial to the smell of her cooking and as he was getting exceedingly hungry, he was keen to get home to his own supper.

"Of course I'll look after the little ones," he said, "but don't be too long."

Away went Nyalango and Apowojjo set about amusing the little ones.

After a little bit of tummy tickling and cooing into their faces, Apowojjo's hunger turned into an ache. All he could think about was the empty void in his stomach and how soon he could fill it. You see what the dragon-fly's mistake had done? Instead of all animals of every kind, loving and trusting each other, now they viewed each other with suspicion and fear and greed and, I hate to say it, as a source of food. So perhaps, in the circumstances, you can understand how this not very nice *rabbit* rabbit, whose impatient stomach was aching with hunger, might suddenly think how tender and succulent were his sister's little babies. No sooner had the thought entered his head, than he had popped one into his mouth and swallowed it.

"Yummy!" he thought. "That was the tastiest morsel I've had in ages," and one by one he began to consume the rest.

He had just reached the last baby, when suddenly his sister came home.

"Apowojjo, Apowojjo! Bring me my babies so that I can feed them."

"Oh no!" gasped Apowojjo! His sister had flopped down under the cool shade of a tree and was waiting to feed her babies. "What shall I do?"

Then he grasped the only remaining baby and with a great display of avuncular affection, carried it tenderly to its mother's arms.

As she suckled her young one she cooed, "Were my little treasures well behaved?"

"Perfect, wonderful, adorable creatures!" replied Apowojjo rubbing his belly.

His sister then handed him the sated infant and asked for the next... and the next... and the next...

At first, Apowojjo got away with bringing the same baby out over and over again, but now, the poor little thing was bloated fit to burst, and Apowojjo knew that any minute now, his sister would realise something was wrong.

"Oh look! Nyang is home!" cried Nyalango. They saw the long, low shape of her crocodile husband swimming home.

"Dearest sister!" cried Apowojjo. "Forgive me for not staying to supper. I must fly. I'll come again soon and visit you. Byeee!" and he fled down to the river bank.

As Nyang's long snout touched the shore, Apowojjo raced up to him and cried, "Please, dear brother-in-law, I've just been visiting my sister and looking after your adorable little ones. Now I'm most terribly late. Be so kind as to ferry me over to the other side."

"Of course, Apowojjo!" exclaimed the crocodile. "Just jump onto my back!"

They were already half way across when Nyalango discovered the awful truth. She came rushing down to the river and stood on the shore wailing and shouting and screaming. "Nyang! Nyang! My evil brother has eaten our babies. Kill him! Kill him!"

But a storm was brewing, and what with the wind whistling over their ears and the water slapping against his body, Nyang didn't quite hear, and thought that his sister was urging him to hurry up and deliver her brother safely to shore. So he swam even faster, and soon Apowojjo was on the far side.

"Cheerio, old chap!" he yelled, and without further ado, sped away into the bush with scarcely a flash of white from beneath his tail.

As Nyang swam back home, he could still hear his wife's dreadful cries. Now he knew something was wrong.

"Our babies, our babies! My wicked brother has eaten our babies!" sobbed Nyalango. "Oh why didn't you stop when I called you? Why didn't you kill him? I want my revenge!" she shrieked.

Nyang's cold crocodile blood nearly froze with anger. Snap, snap, snap went his great, sharp-toothed jaws. "Don't worry, dearest wife. We will have our revenge. Just you see! I'll make sure that Apowojjo dies a terrible death. I'll make sure that there will not be one river, one lake, one stream, one single solitary drinking hole in the whole wide world, where he will be able to drink, without one of us being there ready to snap off his head."

The word went out to every crocodile in the world. Apowojjo is an enemy and must be destroyed.

As Apowojjo wandered furtively across the land, he knew he was in trouble. His mouth was getting more and more dry. His tongue was swelling with thirst and his throat was as parched as a desert. Every time he lowered his head to drink, up came the snip, snap snip jaws of a crocodile.

Apowojjo was getting desperate and thought he would die, when suddenly he had an idea. "Oh Apowojjo!" he sniggered to himself. "What is it a crocodile loves more than anything else in the world?" he chuckled uproariously. "Why," he replied to himself, "the lango fruit, of course!"

His strength had almost run out. Another hour without water and he would die. But he just had enough energy to get to the lango tree. There, he grabbed an armful of fruit and stumbled back towards the river.

He flung himself down on his belly and stuck out his thick, dry tongue towards the precious liquid. It almost touched, when up reared the deadly jaws of a crocodile.

"Snip, snap, snip!"

Apowojjo drew back out of reach, but didn't run away. Instead, he held out some fruit tantalisingly above the crocodile's nose. "Do you know what this is?" he taunted.

The crocodile slammed shut his jaws and looked. Then he parted them again, just a little, because his mouth began watering with desire. "Lango fruit! Lango fruit! Where, oh where did you get it, Apowojjo?"

"That would be telling, wouldn't it!" sneered Apowojjo, "but I tell you what. You let me drink from this water hole, and I'll give you some lango fruit."

The crocodile looked around with a guilty air.

"Who would know this once?" wheedled Apowojjo. "I won't tell anyone. Here… look… it's a ripe juicy one. You can have it, if you let me drink just a few drops to wet my tongue."

"Oh all right!" whispered the crocodile. "Go on then, drink quickly and give me the fruit."

So Apowojjo, with such a triumphant grin, plunged his head into the water and drank and drank until water was almost coming out of his ears.

At first the same crocodile came again and again, allowing Apowojjo to drink in exchange for the fruit. But corruption is like a disease, and like a disease, it soon became known among all the crocodiles, that Apowojjo had a source of lango fruit, and that he was willing to exchange it for water. One by one, the crocodiles found all sorts of reasons to forget how evil Apowojjo was and, in their desire to have the lango fruit, made deals with him.

His brother-in-law, Nyang realised that Apowojjo was getting away with it. He decided that the only way he could get the crocodiles back on his side, was to find out where this lango fruit tree grew.

"Apowojjo! Where is the tree from where you get this fruit?" he pleaded. "If you show it to me, perhaps we can come to some agreement."

Apowojjo was bored with having to collect the fruit each time he wanted a drink, so he said, "All right. I'll show you where the lango tree grows if you promise to let me drink from any watering place in the world whenever I like."

"I promise, I promise!" exclaimed Nyang.

"Very well then, everyone follow me!" ordered Apowojjo.

Two by two, from all the lakes and rivers and streams and watering places came the crocodiles. Every single one of them; young, old, healthy, sick; even those who were blind or deaf or could barely walk. They all came, determined not to miss out on knowing where the lango fruit tree grew. The crocodiles formed a crocodile trail. It stretched as far as the eye could see. Oyajjo, their chief set off in front, while Apowojjo announced that he would lead from the back, keeping pace with the weakest of the weak.

And so they trudged across the dry earth, away from their own kingdom of water.

Apowojjo had found himself a mighty club. Now as they trailed across the land, he took up his club and struck down the last straggling crocodile. A weak old thing with only one eye and three legs.

"Why did you do that?" exclaimed the next with horror.

"Congawa, congawa! He was holding us up! And you do want to get to the lango tree, don't you?"

The crocodile shrugged and said, "I suppose so," and continued walking.

Then Apowojjo clubbed the next and the next, and each time when the one in front protested, Apowojjo cried, "Congawa, congawa! They were holding us up, and you do want to get to the lango tree, don't you?"

And each time, the crocodiles were only too willing to overlook the dreadful deed in their eagerness to get to the delectable fruit. So they hurried on and didn't look back, and Apowojjo was able to kill all the crocodiles one by one, until they were all dead, except for one new-born infant, who just slithered off the track into the long grass.

Apowojjo knew that one had got away. He was furious. He didn't want there to be one single crocodile left in the whole world who might try and stop him drinking from the water hole. So he searched frantically this way and that.

Suddenly, he noticed an Ogworo bird sitting on a tree looking smug.

"Do you know where the last crocodile on earth is hiding?" demanded Apowojjo?

"Of course I do. I saw it all from my branch. But you needn't think I'm telling you," scoffed the bird.

Apowojjo furiously hurled his club at the bird. It tumbled down in a flurry of feathers, and Apowojjo thought he had killed it. "Oh well," he thought, as he stumped away. "It was only a new-born crocodile, and we're miles away from any water. It will surely die in no time at all." So he went away, confident that he had destroyed all his enemies.

But the Ogworo bird wasn't dead at all. He wasn't even hurt. He just flapped away a few loose feathers and then went over to the quivering little baby crocodile who crouched fearfully in the long, dry grass.

"Come on little treasure, let me take you under my wing. We'll soon have you big and strong," and the kindly bird managed to coax the little creature all the way to a river, and here, he nursed it until it grew into a huge, female crocodile, as big as any the world has ever seen.

Of course, God had observed everything that had happened. He wasn't too pleased at the thought of one of his species being wiped out for ever. No jumped-up *rabbit* rabbit was going to wipe out the mighty crocodile. So he sent waves of crocodile energy from the Rough Wind, to wash over the female crocodile. And in the waves, were the spirits of all the other crocodiles, and these spirits entered her body and filled her with eggs.

Soon, every river and lake and stream and watering hole was filled once more with crocodiles, and Apowojjo never ever knew safety again.

"Gi kal konyi way; kipo o nakka Ji ben," cry the warriors to this very day. "United we stand, divided we fall. The strong must protect the weak. We must never copy the greedy crocodile, who was prepared to sacrifice his own race, even his own children, for the sake of greed."

And never, ever say "Congawa!"

By the way, if anyone ever asks you why the Ogworo bird sits so close to the edge of the river, without fear of the crocodile, you know the reason why. Don't you!

8. DIVALI

Hindu festival of lights

Divali falls on a moonless night in late autumn. Preparations start a few days before the actual festival. We pray to Goddess Lakshmi (the goddess of wealth). She demands that the houses are sparkling with purity and cleanliness. The houses are religiously painted and white-washed. Tiled floors are scrubbed clean ready for the Rangoli pattern. Doorsteps are adorned with welcoming Rangoli patterns. After sunset the prayers are said to Lakshmi. Then the celebrations begin. Oil lamps used to be lit in every window, veranda and garden. Gradually we started to light candles instead of clay lamps with oil in them. We wear new, colourful clothes. Delicious foods and sweets are prepared which are shared with friends, relatives and neighbours. The houses glitter with lights. It literally resembles fairyland. Each home has its own firework display with sparklers, rockets and chakris (Catherine wheels). Divali is celebrated throughout India for five days. It is a national festival and holiday time.

Kavita Sharma.

Making a Divali card

Cards and presents are exchanged at Divali time. The greeting inside the card is often Subh Diwali meaning Happy Divali. Messages are frequently written in Punjabi on the left hand page and English on the right.

Diwali Mubarak Gujarati

દીવાળી મુબારક

Shuvodeoali Bengali

শুভ দেওয়ালী

Shub Dipavali Hindi

शुभ दीपावली

Diwali Mubarik Urdu

دیوالی مبارک

The pictures on the cards may be of Lakshmi seated in a lotus flower, Rama and Sita or of diva lamps.

Everyone has some new clothing to celebrate Divali. There is often an evening celebration at the mandir with worship, music, Indian dance and food. A fireworks display recalling the battle between Rama and Ravana is sometimes arranged as part of the festivities.

Rangoli patterns

In many Hindu homes the lights and candles are also lit to welcome the goddess Lakshmi, the wife of Vishnu. Lakshmi is the goddess of good fortune and wealth who is said to visit every Hindu home once a year. By the time Lakshmi visits, all accounts have to be closed and all debts settled marking the end of the year. The new year starts and all family quarrels are forgotten.

In India it is still traditional to decorate the floors with brightly coloured patterns, called Rangoli patterns. The designs are made from natural products and dyes such as rice, flour and water, dry powders such as turmeric, spices and chalk or flower petals. The designs are usually based on flower or leaf shapes.

The Divali festival

The word 'Divali' comes from the Sanskrit word, 'Deepavali' meaning 'clusters of light'.

The Divali festival, one of India's most important and popular festivals, happens to fall towards the end of October or November, when Jews are preparing to celebrate Hanukkah, their light festival, and Christians look forward to Christmas. Children in Britain also remember Guy Fawkes night with bonfires and fireworks, and perhaps it is no accident that these celebrations all take place when the nights are longer and darker.

In India, Divali is celebrated in different ways. The Bengalis know the festival better as the Kali Puja. Kali is the ferocious goddess wife of Lord Shiva. She is the bloodthirsty avenger of enemies and the controller of evil spirits. But she is also the Great Mother who is kind and benevolent, if you revere her properly.

Each Autumn, before the night of the full moon, Bengalis light fourteen oil-filled earthenware lamps to venerate Kali. All over Bengal, these lamps softly flicker through the dark hours. But on the night of the full moon, every kind of light is used to destroy the forces of evil. The whole sky is ablaze with electric lights, candles, lamps and fireworks.

For others, Divali is primarily the festival which celebrates the homecoming of Prince Rama and Sita out of their fourteen year exile in the jungle and his victory over the evil demon king, Ravana.

The story of Rama and Sita

Over two thousand years ago, the epic story known as the Ramayana was set down. It tells of Prince Rama who was the eldest of four sons. His ailing father, the king, decided to abdicate in favour of this popular prince who had recently married the beautiful princess Sita.

The kingdom of Ayodhya was overjoyed, and the people immediately set about preparing for the coronation. The night before the great event, the four queens stood on the palace roof excitedly watching all the festivities below. Queen Kaykai, mother of Bharata, the second eldest son, clapped her hands with pleasure as a procession of decorated elephants, horses and camels paraded by.

Suddenly, a low voice hissed in her ear. "I don't know what you're so pleased about. None of these celebrations is for your son."

Queen Kaykai turned to find her son's old nursemaid, twisting her hands with jealous anger. She had suckled and nursed Prince Bharata and cared for him all through his childhood. She loved him with fierce passion and was made cunning by ambition for him.

"Do you remember when the king was ill?" continued the old woman in a wily voice.

"Yes," murmured Queen Kaykai, "we all thought he was dying."

"He would have died, if it hadn't been for you," hissed the nursemaid. "You saved his life, and for that he made you a solemn promise. Do you remember?"

"Of course I remember," smiled the queen, "but he had no need to make me any such promises. I nursed him back to life because I loved him and it was my duty."

"Ah!" exclaimed the nursemaid. "But he promised that you could have anything that you desired, and a promise is a promise and cannot be broken; it is God's law! Now is the time to make him keep his promise. You can demand that your son, Bharata be crowned king tomorrow instead of Rama."

Thus did these evil words set off a train of events which led, not just to Prince Bharata sitting on the throne of Ayohdya, but to the banishment and fourteen year exile of Prince Rama into the jungle. At his side, went the beautiful Princess Sita, who would not be separated from her beloved husband. His devoted younger brother, Lakshmana, went too. "With me by your side," he said, "You might have a chance of surviving."

The jungle was full of fearful dangers; there were wild animals who could tear them apart and devour them; poisonous snakes and spiders and blood-sucking insects: but most dangerous of all were the demons, who watched the three of them with evil eyes.

King Ravana, the fearsome, ten-headed king of all demons, fell in love with the beautiful Sita, and by evil trickery, kidnapped her and transported her far away to his kingdom on the island of Lanka. He tried to make her love him, but she rejected him with scorn, so he kept her prisoner, humiliated and abused.

For many years, Rama and his faithful brother, Lakshmana, roamed through the perilous jungle, searching desperately for Sita. At last, they reached the kingdom of the monkeys and met the noble Hanuman, son of Vayu, God of the Wind. Using his magic powers, Hanuman flew over to Lanka and found the princess Sita. She was safe and well, though overwrought with grief, because she thought that she would never see Rama again.

Now all the monkeys of the jungle rallied together into an army. With loud war cries, they marched down to the shore and gazed across at the island glittering like a jewel in the ocean. Watching them from afar, the demons sniggered. It's all very well for Hanuman with his magic powers to fly over the ocean, but monkeys can't fly or swim. How could they possibly launch an attack?

But undeterred, the monkeys began collecting rocks and boulders and fallen trees, and with the help of the spirits of the ocean, they began to build a bridge across to the island. The demons watched in amazement, as day by day, the bridge extended further and further towards them. Within only five days, the bridge reached the island shore, and with a roar of triumph, the monkey army, with Rama at their head, surged across.

A terrible battle took place. Hundreds and thousands of demons and monkeys were slain. It seemed as if no one could win. At last, through the smoke of battle, Ravana, King of the demons came face to face with Rama.

Rama aimed arrow after arrow at Ravana's ten heads. But as each head was struck, another grew in its place. It seemed as if Ravana was indestructible. Finally, Rama knew he must use the golden arrow of Brahma. It was his last chance to save Sita and his last chance to destroy this king of darkness. He fitted the sacred arrow, carefully took aim and fired. The arrow thudded into Ravana's heart. Ravana gave a terrible scream; his ten heads rolled in agony, and at last, he thudded to the ground, dead. When the demons saw their master fall, they fled in disarray.

Hanuman went into the dungeons of the palace and found Sita. What a resounding cry of joy echoed over the defeated kingdom as Hanuman handed Sita to her husband and said, "Rama, receive thy wife!"

Now the fourteen years were over. Triumphantly, Rama, Sita and Lakshmana returned to the city of Ayodhya. When the loyal citizens heard they were coming, they lit lamps and hung them all over the city; they outlined the roofs of houses and the sills of windows; they lined the streets and pathways, the terraces and steps. The whole sky was lit up as bright as day to welcome home their rightful king and queen.

From that day on, every year, the homecoming of Rama and Sita is celebrated and known as the Festival of Divali.

Remembering that Rama is an incarnation of Lord Vishnu, the Preserver, his battle with Ravana represents the eternal battle between Good and Evil throughout all eternity.

Jamila Gavin.

Make a diva lamp

You will need some clay, a night light, paints and a brush.

Roll out a ball of clay slightly larger than a table tennis ball.

Gently push your thumb into the ball of clay and smooth out the hole until the night light will fit into it.

Leave the diva shape to dry out. This will take several days.

Decorate the diva lamp using brightly coloured paints.

When the paint is dry, place your candle in the lamp and light it.

Lakshmi and the clever washerwoman

Once upon a time a king and queen lived in a beautiful palace. The Queen was rather spoiled and vain. Every Divali, she would ask her husband for the most expensive presents. Each year, the King gave her whatever she asked for, however difficult it was for him to get it.

One particular year, the Queen had asked for a seven-string necklace of large pearls.

The King sent a thousand divers to the far corners of the earth searching for those pearls. Just before Divali, the divers returned. They had, at great peril to their own lives, found just the right oysters and, from them, pulled out only those rare pearls that were large and perfect.

The grateful King thanked the divers profusely and gave them large sums of money for their labours. He sent the pearls to the royal jeweller to be strung and on Divali morning he was able to present his wife with the gift she desired.

The Queen was jubilant. She put on the necklace and immediately ran to the mirror to admire herself. She turned her head this way and that, convinced that she was, indeed, the most beautiful creature in the whole world.

It was the Queen's custom to go to the river every morning to bathe, accompanied by a bevy of handmaidens. On this particular morning when she got to the river bank, she undressed and, just as she was poised to dive into the water, she remembered that she was still wearing her seven-string necklace of pearls.

So she stopped and took it off, laying it on top of her clothes. "Watch my necklace," she called, as she dived off a rock.

The handmaidens watched the necklace carefully, but something happened which even they were unprepared for. A crow flew down from a nearby tree, picked up the necklace and flew away with it. The handmaidens screamed and shouted but it was no use. The crow had flown out of their sight.

When the Queen found out what had happened she cried with frustration and anger. She went back to the palace and, still sobbing, told the King of her misadventure. The King tried to console her, saying that he would get her a prettier necklace but the Queen pouted and said that she would not be happy until her seven-string necklace was found.

So the King summoned his drummers and heralds. He ordered them to go to every town and village in the kingdom, telling the people

that a reward would be offered to anyone who found the Queen's necklace.

Meanwhile, the crow had flown from the manicured palace grounds to one of the lowliest slum areas. Here he dropped the necklace on the doorstep of a poor washerwoman's hut.

The washerwoman did not live alone. She shared the hut with her constant companion, an old, toothless crone, called Poverty. The two were not particularly fond of each other but they had been together ever since the washerwoman could remember and had become quite used to each other's ways.

As it happened, the two occupants of the hut were away when the crow flew by. The washerwoman was collecting dirty laundry and Poverty, as usual, was accompanying her. On their way home, they passed the village market where they stopped to hear the King's drummers and the proclamation about the Queen's necklace. Poverty began to cackle, "Oh the ways of royalty! What will they lose next? Why do they bother us common people with their antics!"

But the washerwoman was thinking other thoughts. She had never owned any jewellery and wondered how she would look in a seven-string necklace.

When they got home and the washerwoman put her bundles down, the first thing she noticed was the pearl necklace lying on her doorstep. She picked it up and was about to put it on when a thought occurred to her. "I have an errand to run," she told Poverty, "I will be back in a minute." So saying, she rushed off with the necklace and headed straight for the King's palace.

The guards tried to stop her but when she told them what she was carrying, they escorted her directly to the King.

The King was very happy to get his wife's necklace back. He praised the washerwoman for her honesty and then, picking up a large purse containing the reward money, he said, "Here, take this for your pains. It should keep you well fed and well clothed for the rest of your days."

To his surprise, the King found himself being refused. The washerwoman seemed to have something else in mind. She said, "I am a poor, humble washerwoman, Your Majesty. I do not want the money which you are so kindly offering me. There is one favour, however, that I hope you will grant me. Today is Divali. I want you to decree that no one, not even you, will light any oil lamps in his home. Today I want all houses to be dark. All except mine, I want mine to be the only lighted house in the entire kingdom."

The King, grateful that he had got off so lightly, agreed. He sent out his drummers and heralds with the decree as he had promised. He ordered his palace servants to take down all the oil lamps and to put them into storage for the following year.

The washerwoman rushed home, buying as many oil lamps along the way as she could afford. She arranged these carefully outside her hut and waited.

Night fell. The washerwoman lit all her lamps and looked around. The rest of the kingdom to the north, south, east and west, lay in total darkness.

Lakshmi had, of course, left the heavens and was ready to perform her yearly duty of going from house to house, blessing with prosperity all those that were well lit. This year, something was wrong. There were no lights to be seen anywhere. Poor Lakshmi stumbled along in the darkness, from one house to another, but nowhere could she see the slightest trace of a welcoming glimmer.

Suddenly she spotted a glow of bright lights far away in the distance. She began running towards it.

It was the middle of the night when a very exhausted Lakshmi got to the washerwoman's hut. She began pounding on the door, crying, "Let me in, let me in!"

This was the moment that the washerwoman had been waiting for. She called out to Lakshmi, saying, "I will let you in only on the condition that you will stay with me for seven generations." Just then, the washerwoman looked behind her and saw Poverty trying to creep out through the back door. She rushed to the door and locked it. Poverty began to shout, "Let me out, let me out! You know there isn't room in this hut for both Lakshmi and me."

So the washerwoman said, "All right, I will let you go but only on the condition that you do not return for seven generations." Poverty said, "Yes, yes, I will do as you ask. Just let me out of this place. I cannot stand the sight of Lakshmi." At that the washerwoman opened the back door and Poverty rushed out.

Then she hurried to the front door where Lakshmi was pounding desperately and crying,

"Let me in, let me in."

"Only on the condition that you stay with me for seven generations," the washerwoman repeated.

"Yes, yes," said Lakshmi, "I will do anything you ask, only let me in."

And so the poor washerwoman let Lakshmi into her home and it was blessed with wealth and prosperity for seven generations.

Madhur Jaffrey.

Food for Divali

Burfi

Burfi is an Indian sweetmeat eaten at special events. It is usually made from full cream dried milk (khoa), but you can also get a good result using evaporated milk.

4 cups (400g) desiccated coconut
1 cup (200g) granulated sugar
¼ cup (50g) melted butter
1 large tin evaporated milk
4 cups (900ml) water

You can also add nuts, dried fruit or cardamom

Mix the coconut with the evaporated milk.

Boil the sugar and water until it thickens, then lower the heat and add the coconut and milk mixture.

Add the butter very slowly, stirring all the time.

Allow the mixture to thicken in the pan. To vary the basic recipe you can add any fruit, nuts or spices at this stage.

Spread the mixture onto a greased baking tray or plate.

Wait for a few minutes then mark the mixture into squares, it can look attractive if you decorate it with nuts or crystallised fruit.

Leave the burfi to cool completely before you remove it from the tray.

Pakoras:

Pakoras are pieces of vegetable fried in a light spicy batter. It is vital to use chickpea flour which an be found in good wholefoods shops or in oriental food stores. Use small pieces of whatever vegetables are available — experiment with any of these: leek, broccoli, onion, cauliflower, mushroom tops, green beans, carrots, peppers, cucumber, potatoes, courgette or marrow.

1½ cups (300g) chickpea flour
1½ teaspoons salt
½ teaspoon cayenne
1½ teaspoons turmeric
½ teaspoon ground cumin
1½ cups (350ml) water

Instead of the spices above you can use 1 teaspoon garam masala with 1 teaspoon chilli powder.

Mix the dry ingredients in a large bowl. Whisk in about half the water, and very gradually add the rest, beating until there are no lumps.

Coat the vegetables and deep fry carefully in very hot vegetable oil. Fry until golden brown and eat while piping hot with chutney or tomato sauce.

Jalebis:

175g plain flour
Salt
¾ tablespoon baking powder
3 tablespoons natural yoghurt
450g caster sugar
900ml water
1 teaspoon jalebi powder or powdered saffron or turmeric

Oil for deep frying
Chopped pistachio nuts for garnish

This recipe is unsuitable for children to follow because of the safety element involved in boiling water or hot fat. However, the end product is a delicious and different sweetmeat. The children will get their enjoyment from the tasting.

Sift the flour, salt and baking powder into a bowl. Stir in the warm water and then beat in the yoghurt until the batter is smooth.

Cover the bowl with a cloth and leave in a warm place to ferment for eight hours.

Dissolve the sugar in 600ml of water, add the jalebi or saffron powder. Boil until the syrup thickens, remove from the heat and keep syrup warm over a saucepan of hot water.

Heat the oil in a frying pan. Heat the batter in another pan, stirring continuously. The batter should be the consistency of thick cream.

Using a piping bag fitted with a plain nozzle, pipe the batter into the hot oil. Move the nozzle round in circular movements, starting at the centre.

Fry a few jalebis at a time until golden brown all over. Remove with a perforated spoon and drain on kitchen paper. Dip the jalebis into the syrup for at least 15 minutes.

Gently lift the jalebis out of the syrup and sprinkle them with the chopped pistachio nuts.

Jalebis are delicious eaten hot or cold.

V

WINTER

1. FILIPINO FIESTA

Fiesta in the Philippines

The Philippines is caught in its own history; a culture immersed in customs and traditions, festivals, carnivals and other forms of celebrations. Such festivities vary in their intensity depending on their importance and solemnity. The significance of such provides entertainment and an 'excuse' to have fun.

One good example is the 'fiesta' which is a festival celebrated in every town and in barrios (villages). It is a significant occasion where a patron saint is honoured as appointed by the Catholic Church.

In my own hometown 'Pidigan', our fiesta is celebrated on the 8th December in honour of the Immaculate Conception.

A few weeks before the great occasion both the elementary and secondary schools (in our town) prepare a full programme of folk dances, gymnastics and music.

Everyone feels the excitement as new clothing is prepared, pigs and cows or goats are bought to be fattened up and then slaughtered for the great occasion. A couple of days before the big day, bunting lines the streets, and side shows such as the circus start to arrive. Marquees and tents are erected in the town plaza.

Every household takes special care in cleaning all nooks and crannies, in and out of the house.

At the crack of dawn on the 8th December, one wakes up to the squeals of pigs and cows being slaughtered and from that moment, the main centre of activity is in the kitchen where all kinds of food are prepared and cooked. Chicken Adobo and Rellenong Bañgus are two

specialities on this big occasion.

Attending the morning Holy Mass is the first important activity of the day where everyone wears their new suits, dresses and shoes. (I can never forget my first bright orange pair of low-heeled shoes. Looking back now, they were the most horrendous colour, but then at that time, they were the latest fashion.)

As customs would allow, all friends and relatives from other towns are invited beforehand, to attend the fiesta and then join in the highlight of the day which is the 'dinner'. The 'pig on a spit' is the main attraction of the dinner table; the preparation and cooking time of this dish takes about 6 to 8 hours, and one needs to be in constant attendance so as not to undercook or overcook the pig.

The special programme prepared by both schools is then shown to the public and the best performances are awarded by special donations from visiting dignitaries or some wealthy town folk. In the evening there would be a play performed by a theatrical group (Ticong and Ticang), well known around the region for their tear-jerker dramas.

On the whole, fiesta time is one occasion to see the circus and magic stalls, go around the bazaars, visit friends and relatives, watch the different competitions, such as climbing the slippery bamboos with a prize on the top, and generally just having lots of fun.

Tin can lantern

(For older children!) You will need the following:

A big can
Paper, pencil and scissors
Tape
Hammer and nails of different sizes
Wire (for the handle)
Small candle or nightlight
Folded towel or old cushion

1. Fill the can with water and freeze it overnight
2. Cut out a piece of paper which is the right size to fit around the can.
3. Draw a simple design or pattern and then tape the paper around the can.
4. Put the can on its side on an old cushion or folded towel and hammer and nail a little way into the ice along the lines of your design. You can use different sized nails to give variety.
5. When you have finished hammering your design, hammer two 'hanging holes' on either side of the top of the can.
6. Remove the paper and put the can upside down, in a sink until the ice falls out.
7. Finally attach a wire handle to the lantern and place a candle or nightlight inside.

Hang the lantern in a dark place; perhaps outside at night from branches of trees or by the door to greet guests and friends.

Recipes for fiesta

Chicken adobo:

1 medium size chicken cut in pieces
6 crushed cloves of garlic (more if desired)
⅓ cup of white vinegar
1 cup of water
⅓ cup of soy sauce (dark preferred)
Salt and crushed black peppercorns

Put chicken pieces in the saucepan; add the garlic, salt, vinegar, black pepper and water.

Cover the pan and let it boil, lower the heat and simmer for 45 minutes or until there is no more liquid in the pan.

Chicken adobo can be served with boiled or fried rice. (Chicken can be replaced with pork if desired.)

This dish is cooked during town fiestas or special occasions such as weddings or christenings, or as a special treat for the family.

Rellenong baṅgus or stuffed milkfish:

This recipe takes a lot of preparation time but it is worth giving it a try. It is always a special treat to have 'Rellenong Baṅgus' during fiestas and Christmas dinners.

Milkfish or baṅgus is a very tasty fish and once you've eaten one, you'll never forget it!

1 big baṅgus
1 small onion chopped
¼ cup raisins
¼ cup chopped green olives
2 hard boiled eggs
2 ripe tomatoes
¼ cup chopped pickles
1 cup garden peas
¼ cup tomato sauce
2 tablespoons cooking oil
Salt and pepper to taste

Wash the baṅgus and slit an opening at the back. Pound the fish with a rolling pin to loosen the meat without spoiling the skin. Then remove the meat and discard the bones. If bones are not easily removed, put the meat in the liquidizer for 1 minute to crush all the bones. Sauté the garlic with cooking oil, add the onion and tomatoes then put in the baṅgus meat. Then add the rest of the ingredients and season with salt and pepper. When cooked, stuff the mixture into the fish, and sew the slit making the fish look whole again. Fry the fish and serve with rice.

Avocado pear ice cream:

This is made when avocado pears are in season in the Philippines. It is a special treat to make for birthdays, Christmas or fiesta celebrations.

5 avocado pears (mashed)
4 cups milk
1 cup white sugar (brown if preferred)

Boil the milk, then cool. Cut open the avocado pears and scoop out the flesh and mash it to a pulp.

Put the mashed avocado pears, sugar and (cooled down) milk in the mixer, and churn it for 10 to 15 minutes. Put the mixture in the freezer for ½ hour. Then stir it again. Put it back in the freezer until firmly set.

2. FIRST SNOWFALL AND MOTHER HOLLE

Mother Holle

When the first heavy frost comes, or snowflakes fly, some say these are the white feathers shaken out of Mother Holle's featherbed...

Once upon a time, a long time ago, there lived a widow and her two daughters. The widow had been married twice; her own daughter was rather spoiled and disagreeable with a scowl which made her not very pleasant to look at! The step-daughter was kindly and hard-working, having already suffered in her young life. Unfortunately the widow much favoured her own daughter, treating the other as a housemaid.

Every day the step-daughter had to clean, cook, and then sit outdoors spinning. Her fingers were always sore and often bled. One day she bent to wash blood off her spindle in the well, but it slipped and fell in. She was scolded for this by her step-mother who shrieked, "You dropped it, foolish child! You must go down after it yourself!"

The poor girl reached desperately too far into the well and tumbled in, sinking to the bottom. But this was no ordinary well — for when she next opened her eyes she was in a lovely meadow full of sunshine and wild flowers. She rose and wandered, spellbound, until she came to a baker's oven full of bread.

The bread called out to her, "Take me out or I shall be burnt to cinders!" So she carefully removed the loaves and set them down. Walking on, she came to an apple tree laden with rosy fruit. "Shake me, shake me!" It called to her, "My apples are quite ripe." So she did.

The girl walked on until she came to a path of cobblestones which led to a tiny house with shutters on the windows. In the doorway sat an old woman wrapped in a cloak with a face as wrinkled and old as time itself. "Don't be afraid, child," said the elderly soul. "Come help me with my chores. You may shake my featherbed until all the downy feathers fly. For then it snows, as I am Mother Holle!"

She spoke so kindly that the girl agreed to help, and shook the bed so that feathers flew like snowflakes everywhere. She helped in every way, and was well fed in return. But before long she grew homesick. "You have served me well and faithfully," said Mother Holle. "You may return home if this is your wish, and I will lead you to the other world myself." She took her by the hand to an open door and as the girl crossed the threshold back into her world, a shower of gold covered her! "This is a reward for your labours," smiled the old woman, placing the lost spindle in her hand, as well.

You can imagine how she was welcomed home with her gold! But her stepmother's first thought was to secure for her own daughter such riches! Down the well the other sister was pushed and the spindle thrown in for good measure! She, too, found herself in the beautiful meadow and walked to the baker's oven. "Take me out or I shall be burnt to cinders!" called the bread. But this girl put her hands on her hips and snarled "I wouldn't burn my fingers on your crusts! Burn yourself!"

On she went, coming to the apple tree. "Shake me. Shake me," it called, "my apples are ripe!" The girl tossed back her head and answered "They will fall off in their own time, silly tree."

When she came to the cobblestone path the girl eagerly ran up to the old woman and offered to be her maid. She worked hard her first day, shaking the big featherbed and thinking of gold. The second day she slowed down, for she was not used to doing chores! The third day she pouted all morning and did nothing. Mother Holle dismissed her, and the girl thought now she would get her reward! She was led to the same door as her sister had been, but instead of a rain of gold, a shower of toads fell upon her! Mother Holle handed her the spindle.

The girl ran home, toads hopping off her all the way. When she got home, her step-mother had to think again!

Mother Holle's cookie house

Plan the size of the house according to the sizes of your baking dishes. You will need to cut two triangles and two roof sections from the cookie slabs. The dimensions shown here were easily obtained from this recipe with quite a bit left over for sampling and other construction projects. Best of all, when assembled, the size of house fits nicely onto an average platter with room to spare for landscaping.

Cut paper patterns to be used in making the house.

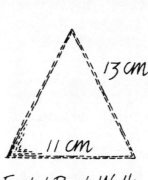

Front & Back Walls   Roof

6 cups (1.2 kilos) wholewheat flour
1 cup (200g) sugar
2 tablespoons baking powder
2 teaspoons cinnamon
1 teaspoon ground cloves
¼ teaspoon nutmeg
¼ teaspoon cardamom
Pinch of salt
1 tablespoon grated lemon peel
¾ cup (150g) honey
¼ cup (50g) butter
⅓ cup (85ml) lemon juice
1 egg and 1 egg yolk

Preheat the oven to 325°F, 160°C, Gas Mark 3.

In a large bowl sift together all of the dry ingredients. In a small bowl, beat together all of the liquid ingredients. Make a well in the centre of the dry mixture. Pour in the liquid mixture. Mix with spoon and hands until all ingredients are combined into a stiff dough.

Lightly grease straight-sided baking dishes (two or three, depending on their size). Smooth onto the bottom of each dish a layer of waxed paper which extends up the sides but not the ends of the dish. Press and roll dough into the dish to a uniform thickness of about 1cm (½"), making the top surface as smooth as possible. Bake for about 30 minutes or until light brown.

Remove from oven and cool for no more than 5 minutes. Holding one edge of waxed paper,

177

gently ease 'cookie' from baking dish to counter. Using paper patterns, immediately cut out walls and roof with a sharp knife. Allow to cool completely.

On a plate or wooden base, outline the basic shape of the house with thick rolls of 'snow'. This acts as mortar for setting on the walls and roof. It also serves to join the walls and roof together and to paste the decorations to the house. When the house is assembled, use any extra snow to create a chimney or an interesting landscape.

Snow:

3 egg whites
¾ cup honey (200ml)
3 cups milk powder (750ml)
3 cups finely ground coconut (750ml)
3 teaspoons vanilla (15ml)
1½ teaspoons fresh lemon juice (7.5ml)

Beat egg white with honey until foamy. Cook, stirring constantly over medium heat until mixture reaches thickness of custard. Remove from heat. Add milk powder, coconut, vanilla and lemon juice; mix to a very thick paste. This can

be rolled in slightly dampened hands to make snow drifts on the roof, outlines for doors and windows and beads of paste for sticking on the decorations and for joining the house sections together. (Complete the decorating of all sections before assembling the house.) Topping this 'snow' with unsweetened coconut gives an airier, whiter effect.

Create patterns and shapes with seeds such as sesame and sunflower, almonds and other nuts, dried apricots, pineapple, raisins, dates and so on. For other decorations, melt some carob chips with a few drops of water over a low heat; pour them onto a surface covered with waxed paper and refrigerate until cool enough to cut easily into desired shapes.

Variation:

Shingles of toasted flakes of coconut will help adapt this house to a spring, summer or autumn setting.

Susan Smith.

SNOW HAS FALLEN

Jehanne Mehta

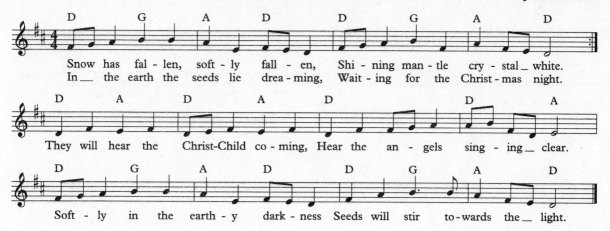

Snow has fal - len, soft - ly fall - en, Shi - ning man - tle cry - stal — white.
In — the earth the seeds lie drea - ming, Wait - ing for the Christ - mas night.

They will hear the Christ-Child co - ming, Hear the an - gels sing - ing — clear.

Soft - ly in the earth - y dark - ness Seeds will stir to - wards the — light.

179

3. WINTER BAKING

Children enjoy making and consuming these goodies on cold days when 'outside' doesn't particularly beckon.

Gingerbread people

½ cup (115ml) oil
½ cup (115ml) runny honey
½ cup (115ml) water
Wholewheat flour
1 teaspoon salt
1 teaspoon allspice
1 teaspoon ground ginger
½ teaspoon ground cloves
½ teaspoon cinnamon
Raisins, currants and nuts for decoration

Preheat the oven to 350°F, 180°C, Gas Mark 4. Grease several baking sheets.

Over a low heat, mix together the oil, honey and water. Remove from the heat and stir in enough wholewheat flour to make a thick batter. Add the salt and spices and then add more flour to make a stiff dough. Chill the dough for half an hour in the refrigerator, then roll out on a floured board.

If you don't have any gingerbread men cutters, make your own shape out of thick cardboard and cut the shapes from the dough by scoring round your shape with a sharp knife.

Before baking, use raisins, currants and nuts to make the eyes, nose, mouth and buttons of each gingerbread person.

Bake for about 15 minutes, or until deep golden brown. Leave the shapes to cool on the baking trays for several minutes before transferring to a wire rack to dry out completely.

Chocolate cookies

¾ cup (150g) butter
⅓ cup (70g) caster sugar
2 tablespoons sweetened condensed milk
Several drops vanilla essence
1 cup (200g) self-raising flour
²/₃ cup (100g) cooking chocolate, grated

Preheat the oven to 325°F, 160°C, Gas Mark 3. Grease two baking trays.

Cream the butter and sugar together until light and fluffy.

Beat in the condensed milk with the vanilla essence.

Gently fold the flour and grated chocolate into the mixture.

Drop the mixture in spoonfuls onto greased baking trays, allowing room for spreading.

Bake in a pre-heated oven for about 12 minutes, until golden brown. Cool on the trays for 2 – 3 minutes before transferring to a wire rack to cool completely.

Nutty oatmeals

¾ cup (150g) butter (softened)
½ cup (100g) caster sugar
½ cup (100g) brown sugar
2 teaspoons vanilla flavouring
2 eggs
¾ cup (150g) plain flour
½ teaspoon salt
¼ teaspoon bicarbonate of soda
3 cups (300g) rolled oats
½ cup (50ml) chopped hazelnuts

Preheat the oven to 350°F, 180°C, Gas Mark 4.
Grease two baking trays.

Beat the butter, sugars and vanilla flavouring
together in a large bowl until light and fluffy.

Add the eggs, beating thoroughly.
Sift the flour, salt and soda into the creamed
mixture. Fold in ¾ of the oats with the
hazelnuts.

Roll heaped teaspoonsful of the mixture in the
remaining oats, and place on the baking tray,
allowing room for spreading.

Bake for about 8 minutes, or until golden
brown. Cool on the trays for 2 – 3 minutes, then
transfer to a wire rack to cool completely.

Grandma Addie's apple bread

1 cup (200g) unrefined white flour
1 cup (200g) wholewheat flour
¾ cup (100g) bran or bran cereal
1 teaspoon baking powder
1 teaspoon bicarbonate of soda
1 teaspoon caraway seeds
¼ teaspoon salt
½ cup (100g) butter
²/₃ cup (140g) sugar
Grated rind of ½ orange or lemon
2 eggs
2 cups (300g) coarsely grated apple
1¹/₃ cups (140g) coarsely chopped walnuts

Preheat oven to 350°F, 180°C, Gas Mark 4.
Grease and flour 1 large loaf pan.

Combine the flour, baking powder, bicarbonate
of soda, caraway seeds and salt in a small bowl.
In a large bowl cream together the butter and
sugar with the orange or lemon rind until light
and fluffy.

Beat in the eggs one at a time.

Fold in the flour mixture with the apple and
walnuts. You will now have a soft batter. Pour
this into your loaf tin and bake in the preheated
oven for about 55 minutes. The loaf is ready
when a skewer inserted into its centre comes out
clean.

Cool the loaf on a wire rack and eat spread with
butter.

Special candies

More complicated to make, these candies are good presents or they will grace a special occasion.

Penuche:

1½ cups (300g) granulated sugar
1 cup (200g) brown sugar
⅓ cup (75ml) single cream
⅓ cup (75ml) milk
2 tablespoons butter or margarine
1 teaspoon vanilla essence
½ cup (50g) broken walnuts or pecan nuts
  (optional)

Before you start, butter the sides of a heavy high-sided 4 pint (2 litre) saucepan. Then grains of sugar cannot cling to the sides of the pan and form crystals, and your fudge will be an even consistency

Place the sugars, cream, milk and butter in the saucepan. Heat over a medium heat, stirring all the time, until the sugar is all dissolved and the mixture begins to boil.

If you have a sugar thermometer cook until the mixture reaches 238°C, stirring only if the mixture starts to stick to the base or sides of the pan. At this temperature the fudge will have reached the softball stage. If you don't have a thermometer, test by dropping a small teaspoon of mixture into a bowl of cold water. If it forms soft balls in the water it is ready!

Immediately remove the pan from the heat and cool, without stirring, for about 10 minutes until the mixture is lukewarm.

Then add the vanilla essence and beat vigorously until the mixture becomes very thick and stops looking shiny.

Quickly stir in the nuts and spread the fudge in a shallow buttered pan.

Score the fudge while it is still warm, and cut and store when it is completely cold.

Quick walnut or pecan penuche:

½ cup (100g) butter or margarine
1 cup (200g) brown sugar
2 cups (400g) caster sugar
¼ cup (55ml) milk
1 cup (100g) chopped walnuts or pecan nuts

Melt the butter in a heavy based saucepan. Add the brown sugar and cook over a low heat for 2 minutes, stirring all the time. Add the milk and continue cooking, still stirring, until the mixture comes to boiling point.

Remove the pan from the heat and, when it has cooled, gradually add the caster sugar until the mixture is the consistency of fudge.

Stir in the chopped nuts and spread the mixture on a buttered tray. Chill in the fridge and cut into squares when solid.

4. CHANUKAH

Jewish festival of lights

The name of this festival may be written as *Chanukah, Chanucah or Hanukkah*.

Chanukah starts on the 25th of the Jewish month of Kislev which is usually in December.

The festival celebrates the defeat of the Greeks by Judas Maccabaeus and his followers and the restoration and cleansing of the temple in Jerusalem. The focus of the festival is the lighting of the eight Chanukah candles during the eight days of the festival.

The usual seven branched candlestick, the menorah, is replaced by one with eight or even

During the festival parties are held and presents are given to the children. Some families give their children a small gift on each of the eight days of Chanukah. This is the time when warming, filling dishes are served to families and friends. Dishes such as potato latkes and rich fruit puddings with sauces and trifles.

The children often play with a special Chanukah spinning top called a driedel. Usually a pile of sweets or nuts are heaped in the middle of the table. The rules are simple. The Hebrew letters on each side of the driedel represent an instruction. The top has four sides and the way it falls tells the players who has won or lost the sweets and nuts. It is said that the four Hebrew letters on each side of the driedel have a magical quality because they are the initial letters of the Hebrew sentence that means, "A great miracle happened here."

nine branches. The nine branched candlestick holds a central or 'servant' candle which is lit and used each day to light the other eight candles. The eight candles represent the eight days the everlasting lamp went on burning. On the first night of Chanukah the children wait for the first three stars to appear in the night sky. The 'servant' candle is lit and from this the first candle of Chanukah is lit. As the candle is lit, thanks are offered to God for saving the Jews from their enemies. The next night two candles are lit from the servant candle. On the third day the servant candle and three candles burn and so on until on the eighth day of the festival eight candles and the servant candle are ablaze.

The first Chanukah celebration

Nearly 2000 years ago in the land of Israel, many Jewish people lived, worked and worshipped together. They worked hard growing crops and looking after their animals for six days every week but every seventh day they rested because they believed that God wanted the seventh day to be a rest day. In the city of Jerusalem, in the land of Israel, there was a magnificent temple and in the temple was a special lamp which glowed with light both night and day.

Unfortunately a cruel, greedy king decided that he would capture the land of Israel for himself. In fact he wanted to capture the whole world. The king sent soldiers to fight but the Israelites led by a man called Mattathias and his five sons encouraged everyone to join them and to fight. After a fierce battle the soldiers were defeated but Mattathias knew that more soldiers would come to fight them, so he led his people right up into the hills. Many other people climbed up into the hills to join them, they all lived in deep caves which were in the hills. Each day they made bows and arrows to attack their enemies with. Every night they surprised the soldiers by attacking them in the dark.

The fighting went on for two years and Mattathias lay dying. He called his five sons, Eleazor, John, Jonathan, Simon and Judas together and told them that he had chosen Judas to be the Maccabee, the trusted leader whom everyone would follow to victory.

After his father's death, Judas Maccabaeus led his people into a fierce battle which they won. Their enemies were driven away from the hills and the people were able to return to their homes.

When everyone saw how the temple in Jerusalem had been defaced they decided to work together to tidy and clean it up. Many parts of the temple had to be rebuilt or repaired, including the special lamp which had glowed with light both night and day. A celebration was organised when order had been restored to the temple but an important part of the celebration was to relight the special lamp of God. A great search took place for some oil to light the lamp. Only a drop of oil to last for one night could be found. A messenger was sent immediately to fetch some more oil but they knew the journey would take him eight days, four days there and four days back again; everyone knew the light would not continue to burn for long enough.

The celebrations commenced. The lamp was lit with the drop of oil and everyone gathered together with cymbals, drums and harps to play and sing God's praises. The flame continued to burn all day and all night and for the whole of the next day and night. In fact it seemed to burn more brightly as each day passed.

On the eighth day, when the messenger returned with the supply of oil, the special lamp of God was still burning brilliantly. Another of God's miracles had occurred.

Chanukah candlestick

Great care must always be taken when children are exposed to a naked flame. A simple Chanukah candlestick can be reproduced by placing a line of nine night lights or nine candles bedded into a ball of plasticine onto a strip of wood which has been sprayed with gold paint. The instructions on the spray can must always be carefully followed.

A 'safe' Chanukah candlestick:

A safer version of the Chanukah candlestick can be reproduced by drawing or painting the candlestick onto a large sheet of paper. The picture is then mounted on a wall. Each day a paper flame is added to the picture until on the eighth day of Chanukah all eight candles and the servant candle are 'lit' without the risk of burning or fire.

A spinning dreidel (Chanukah top)

Cut out a simple cardboard shape, copy the four Hebrew letters onto your dreidel and pierce a hole in the centre to take a short pencil. Happy spinning!

The four Hebrew letters to put on the dreidel:

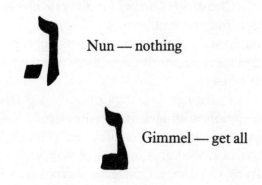

Nun — nothing

Gimmel — get all

Hey — half

Shin — shove in

Recipes for Chanukah

Safety note:

Children do the mixing.
Adults do the frying.
Everyone enjoy!

Potato latkes:

6 large potatoes
1 onion
2 eggs, beaten
Salt and pepper
Flour to bind the mixture

Grate the potatoes and the onion, then stir in the eggs and the salt and pepper.

Thicken this mixture with flour until it is the consistency of a thick batter.

Heat two tablespoons of oil per batch in a frying pan and drop large spoonfuls of the batter into the pan. When the latkes are browned at the edges, turn them over and fry the other side.

Drain on kitchen paper and serve hot with apple sauce, cranberry sauce, yoghurt or simply with a side salad.

To vary the recipe, try adding a finely chopped apple or a few tablespoons of chopped parsley before frying.

Chanukah pudding:

This is a rich fruited steamed pudding which is lighter than a traditional English plum pudding. The advantage of this recipe is that although it has good keeping qualities it can be eaten on the day it is made.

½ cup (100g) margarine
½ cup (100g) soft brown sugar
½ cup (100g) plain flour
¼ teaspoon salt, nutmeg and mixed spice
1 small apple, peeled, cored and grated
1 orange, grated peel and juice
⅔ cup (100g) breadcrumbs
1 cup (100g) raisins
1½ cups (150g) sultanas
2 cups (200g) currants
⅓ cup (50g) mixed peel
⅓ cup (50g) chopped almonds
2 tablespoons brandy
4 tablespoons strong beer

Melt the margarine and brown sugar together, sift flour with salt and spices. Beat all ingredients together in a large bowl. Divide the mixture into two equal parts. Place in two 1 litre pudding basins which have been well greased. Cover with a double thickness of greaseproof paper and then with foil. Each pudding should be steamed for 6 hours. Alternatively the puddings can be cooked more quickly in a microwave oven. Cover the pudding basins with cling film. Pierce the top. Cook puddings individually. Heat on ¾ power for 5 minutes, rest for 3 minutes, heat on power 7 for a further 5 minutes, rest for 20 minutes. Turn out and serve.

(Adjustments may have to be made according to the heating capacity of the microwave oven being used.)

5. CHRISTINGLE

Christingle celebration

Adapted from a custom in the Moravian Church, Christingle is a celebration which offers simple but strong visual symbolism to remember God's gifts. In the Christian tradition the greatest of these gifts was the sending of Jesus. He came into the world as a baby, to grow to manhood and then give his life for the world. So the Christingle Celebration also provides an opportunity to think about less fortunate children and it is usual to offer gifts of prayers and money as a positive contribution to their well-being.

The Christingle Celebration is very adaptable and appeals to all ages. It can take place anywhere; community or village hall, church, school or cathedral at any time of the year; Advent, Christmas, Candlemas, Epiphany,

Easter or just at a 'quiet time' in the church year. It can take place at any time of day, although using lighted Christingles in the late afternoon or evening, in a darkened building, creates a beautiful and memorable effect.

What is a Christingle?

Christingle means 'Christ-light'. The orange represents God's love in the creation of the world.

The cocktail sticks represent God's love in the four seasons of the year.

The fruit and sweet represent God's love in providing the fruits of the earth.

The lighted candle represents God's love in sending Jesus, 'the light of the world'.

The red ribbon represents God's love in the death and resurrection of Jesus.

At the first Christingle service, held on Christmas Eve 1747 at Marienborn, formerly Moravia, the pastor, John de Watteville, encouraged the children to take their Christingle home to relight it and place it in their window to show the light of Christ to passers-by.

How to make a Christingle

1. Take an orange and cut a small cross in the top.
2. Fasten a piece of red ribbon around the middle of the orange and secure with sticky tape.
3. Place a 3″ square of silver foil over the cut in the orange, then take a 4″ candle, place it on top of the foil and then push it firmly into the cut.
4. Put a selection of nuts (peanuts in shells are perfect) raisins, sultanas, cherries or soft sweets on to four cocktail sticks, and insert into the orange evenly near the base of the candle. Make sure the exposed ends of the sticks are covered with a piece of fruit or sweet.

During the Christingle celebrations lighted Christingles are handed out to the children in the service, and they form a procession past the rest of the congregation.

Once seated again much surreptitious nibbling is indulged in by the smallest children before the end of the service, making it a most enjoyable experience for everyone!

Ann Felce.

WINTER SOLSTICE

Jehanne Mehta

1. It's four o'clock and it's al-most dark, The dark-ness falls so soon to-day; The swings are emp-ty in the park Cold win-ter's on its way. But it's time to pass a-round the bowl and it's light-ing up time in my soul For the win-ter sol-stice. But ev-'ry star is list-en-ing To hear what mu-sic we shall bring To the win-ter sol-stice.

Verses 1 & 2

Verses 3 & 4

2. The leaves are trodden on the ground —
So many hopes have fluttered down;
Sometimes I don't know where I'm bound
And the path is hard to see.
But if trees could talk then they would tell
How the leaves were blazing as they fell
With hidden fire.

3. The doors are shut and the curtains drawn;
Cold winter locked out in the street.
The hours seem endless to the dawn
And the stars so far away.
But every star is listening,
To hear what music we shall bring
To the winter solstice.

4. The seed lies buried in the ground,
The longest night will soon be done,
As the year begins another round
The seed begins to grow.
Then the dawn will chase the dark away
And the bells ring out the live long day,
On Christmas morning.

6. CHRISTMAS

Christmas Day

Christmas, 25th December, takes its name from the old English *Cristes Maesse* or *Christ Mass* and may in part find its origins in the ancient festival of the winter solstice. The birth of the Christ Child was meant to bring light into a world of darkness. For Christians this day marks the coming of the Son of God to earth in human form, born of Mary, and the greatest possible reason for celebration.

Advent, or the 'coming' precedes Christmas Day by the time span of four previous Sundays/weeks and is a time of conscious anticipation. In many homes and churches an Advent wreath is hung, made of fir and adorned with four candles. One candle is lit on the first Advent Sunday, two on the next, and so forth until all four burn for Christmas Eve. This is a time for decorating, baking, and exchanging cards. It is also a time for seasonal music and plays based on the Biblical account of the nativity.

Although angels in full heavenly glory play their part in the Christmas story, the nativity stresses the humble origins of Jesus on earth. His human parents, Joseph the carpenter and Mary, must travel to Bethlehem to pay taxes. They go on foot and with a donkey, and Mary is heavily pregnant. On arrival there is no room in hostels or inns for them. The only shelter is a manger, a stall of hay and straw near ox and ass. There, in the stillness of night and under a starry sky, the birth takes place. Shepherds nearby are alerted by angelic singing, and further afield wise men from the East have a magnificent star to guide them as they seek the king predicted by scripture and astrological scholars.

Traditional versions of the Christmas story often took their starting point as the Garden of Eden itself, and the battle between good and evil which culminated with Lucifer's banishment from heaven and earth to his new realm and role as Satan. He is foiled in his later attempt to find and corrupt the Christ babe — by the goodness and strength of the Archangel Michael, by the honesty and clear thinking of the shepherds, by the purity and innocence that birth represents. So it is that midnight of

Christmas Eve has its own special quality and legends. Some say it is a time when animals can speak and kneel, themselves, in reverence. Others say it is a time of miracles and hope; when selfless giving is rewarded in heavenly ways.

The following is an extract from a classic Spanish shepherds tale of Christmas.

The shepherds

The star overhead lighted the way into the stable. Within they found a young woman, very fair, and on the straw beside her a small, new-born child. Benito spoke the questions that were in the minds of all: "What is thy name, woman?"

"They call me Mary."

"And his — the child's?"

"He is called Jesus."

Benito knelt. "*Nene Jesús* — Baby Jesus, the angels have sent us to worship thee. We bring what poor gifts are ours. Here is a young cockerel for thee." Benito laid it on the straw beside the child, then rose and called: "Andrés, it is thy turn."

Andres knelt. "I, Andrés, bring thee a lamb." He put it with the cockerel, rose, and said: "Miguel, give thine."

Miguel knelt. "I bring thee a basket of figs, little one. Carlos, thy turn."

Carlos knelt and held out shepherd-pipes. "I have made them. Thou shalt play on them when thou art grown. Juan, what hast thou?"

Juan knelt. "Here is some cheese — goats' cheese."

In turn they knelt, each shepherd, until all but Esteban, the boy, had given his gift. "Alas,

Nene Jesús, I have little for thee. But here are the ribbons from my cap. Thou likest them, yes? And now I make a prayer: 'Bless all shepherds. Give us to teach others the love for all gentle and small things that is in our hearts. Give us to see thy star always on this, the night of thy birth. And keep our eyes lifted eternally to the far hills.'"

And having made the prayer, and all having given their gifts, the shepherds departed into the night, singing.

Ruth Sawyer, *The Long Christmas*.

CHRISTMAS DAY AND THE BELLS

Jehanne Mehta

1. Christ-mas day and the bells are ring - ing ____ Come and hear the an - gels _ sing - ing ____ Come and hear, ____ Come and hear, ____ Come and hear, ____ hear, ____ Come and hear. ____

2. Come and see the maiden Mary,
And on her breast the new born baby.
Come and see, come and see, come and see.

3. Come and feel the joy that His coming
Brings to the world this Christmas morning.
Come and feel, come and feel, come and feel it.

4. Come and savour the taste of freedom,
For now we're free to enter the Kingdom,
Come and taste, come and taste, come and taste.

5. Incense bears the smell of devotion;
He offers love to the whole of creation.
He offers love, He offers love, He offers love.

6. Christmas Day and the bells are ringing.
Come and hear the angels singing.
Come and hear, come and hear, come and hear.

The fir tree

When you stand round the Christmas tree and look longingly at the toys hanging from the prickly branches, does it not occur to you to ask why it is always this particular tree that is so honoured at Christmas? The dark green fir looks so majestic when laden with bright toys and lit up by Christmas candles, that perhaps it is not easy to believe that it is the most modest of trees. But so it is, and because of its humility it was chosen to bear Christmas gifts to the children. This is the story:

When the Christ Child was born, all people, animals, trees, and other plants felt that a great happiness had come into the world. And truly, the Heavenly Father had sent with the Holy Babe his blessings of peace and goodwill to all. Every day people came to see the sweet Babe, bringing presents in their hands. By the stable wherein lay the Christ Child stood three trees, and as the people came and went under their spreading branches, they thought that they, too, would like to give presents to the Child.

Said the Palm, "I will choose my biggest leaf and place it as a fan beside the manger to waft soft air to the Child."

"And I", said the Olive, "I will sprinkle sweet-smelling oil over him."

"What can I give to the Child?" asked the Fir.

"You?" said the others. "You have nothing to offer. Your needles would prick the wee Babe, and your tears are sticky."

This made the poor Fir very unhappy indeed, and it said, sadly, "Yes, you are right. I have nothing that would be good enough to offer to the Christ Child."

Now, quite near to the trees had stood an Angel, who had heard all that had passed. He

was moved to pity the Fir, who was so lowly and without envy of the other trees, and he resolved to help it.

High in the dark of the heavens the stars were beginning to twinkle, and the Angel begged some of the little ones to come down and rest upon the branches of the Fir. This they were glad to do, and their silvery light shone among the branches just like Christmas candles. From where he lay the Christ Child could see the great dark evening world and the darker forms of the trees keeping watch, like faithful guardians, beside the open door of the stable; and to its delight the fir tree saw the face of the Babe illumined with a heavenly smile as he looked upon the twinkling lights.

The Christ Child did not forget the lovely sight, and long afterwards, he bade that to celebrate his birthday there should be placed in every house a fir tree, which might be lit up with candles to shine for the children as the stars shone for him on his first birthday.

Was not the fir tree richly rewarded for its meekness? Surely there is no other tree that shines on so many happy faces!

German traditional.

Caribbean Christmas

Christmas is still one of the most popular festivals to be celebrated in the Caribbean. Like most countries round the world it is a heady mixture of secular and religious, old and new traditions.

Because of the warm climate all year round, most of the celebrating takes place outdoors, literally on the streets in some cases as in the Jonkunnu processions of Jamaica.

In Dominica there is a village tradition of 'sewinal' singing in the week before Christmas. It is a form of door to door serenading accompanied by a band with musical instruments such as guitar, accordion, drum, forks, spoons and old cans. The sewinal songs were creole songs influenced by the French around the theme of driving out the devil from homes in preparation for the coming of Christ.

Around the 1920s, English Christmas carols were introduced but they tended to be sung mainly at church services. The sewinals changed from the original religious context to fun and frolic as people became more interested in singing for their supper, so to speak. The serenaded hosts would invite the singers in, offering them festive food and drink. The last big 'sewinal' would take place after midnight mass where most households remained awake feasting and dancing.

Jonconnu:

The children could make simple, colourful masks depicting animals, book or cartoon characters. Using percussive instruments they could sing the 'Chrismus a come' song, inventing other items of clothing or jewelry to ask of the spectators.

CHRISMUS A COME

Traditional

1. Chris-mus a come, me wan me la - ma,
Chris-mus a come, me wan me la - ma,
Chris-mus a come, me wan me deg-ge-day,
Chris-mus a come, me wan me deg-ge-day.

2. Pretty, pretty gal, me wan me lama,
   Pretty, pretty gal, me wan me lama,
   Pretty, pretty gal, me wan me deggeday,
   Pretty, pretty gal, me wan me deggeday.

3. Not a shoe to me foot, me wan me lama,
   Not a shoe to me foot, me wan me lama,
   Pretty, pretty gal, me wan me deggeday,
   Pretty, pretty gal, me wan me deggeday.

4. Not a hat to me head, me wan me lama,
   Not a hat to me head, me wan me lama,
   Pretty, pretty gal, me wan me deggeday,
   Pretty, pretty gal, me wan me deggeday.

5. Not a bangle to me han, me wan me lama,
   Not a bangle to me han, me wan me lama,
   Pretty, pretty gal, me wan me deggeday,
   Pretty, pretty gal, me wan me deggeday.

Lama — *presents*.
Deggeday — *finery*.

The singing can be accompanied by any or all of the suggested reggae rhythms. Recorders and rhythm instruments can introduce the song by playing once through the melody. Once the singing has begun, recorders can be used again, either accompanying the singers or playing the melody between some of the verses.

New verses can be added and children might enjoy making masks and improvising dances to the music.

Bass drum, tambour

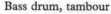

Guitar

Triangle or claves

Congas (or bass guitar)

Bongos

Maracas or cabasa

Christmas food and drink

Rosamund Grant's "Conversations with my mother on Christmas food and drink."

Christmas food and drinks — turkey, ham, roast pork and 'garlic pork' — cakes and sweets, such as 'black cake', 'guava cheese', tamarind balls — lots of rum punches, rice wine, 'fly', ginger beer, jamoon and sorrel drink.

The cake is 'set' from October — the dried fruit, ground and put in a Dutch earthenware jar and to this is added wine, rum, spices, nuts and dried grated orange peel; the important thing is to 'set' it, for a long time, even a year.

A week or so before Christmas the 'black cake' is baked, filling the house with a wonderful aroma.

Christmas meant two extra special treats: ice-apples and grapes. Our Muslim neighbours who were shop-keepers, presented our family with a dish of huge Canadian red apples, always very cold and crisp — not available in the Caribbean, but specially imported for Christmas.

Ham is imported, it arrives sealed in a 'jacket' of tar and on the inside it is wrapped in muslin. It is ceremoniously opened, two days before Christmas, when it is soaked overnight, decoratively studded with cloves and boiled or baked.

A little tradition we have, a few weeks before Christmas, is planting paddy (which makes rice) into little glass containers and by Christmas time, fresh green rice plants, decorate the house.

Rosamund Grant, from *Caribbean and African Cookery*.

Caribbean Christmas cake

My mother's recipe deserves not to be secret any longer and I am sure will be eaten all the year round. This cake is also known as Black Cake. An alternative to marinating the fruits is to bake with 150ml (¼ pint) of sherry and sprinkle the cake, when baked, with another 150ml (¼ pint) of sherry. This cake is surprisingly light. The grinding or liquidising of the fruits is usually appreciated by those of us who don't like meeting up with too many whole raisins and currants, etc. Use muscavado sugar.

Serves 12 or more:

450g (1lb) currants
450g (1lb) raisins
225g (8oz) prunes, stoned
100g (4oz) citron or mixed peel
5ml (1 teaspoon) ground spices
60ml (4 tablespoons) rum or brandy
300ml (½ pint) wine or sherry
450g (1lb) butter or margarine
450g (1lb) self-raising flour
400g (14oz) dark cane sugar
10 large or 12 medium eggs
2.5ml (½ teaspoon) almond essence, to taste
Finely chopped nuts (optional)

Suggested conversion:

4 cups currants
4 cups raisins
2 cups stoned prunes
¾ cup mixed peel
1 teaspoon ground spices
4 tablespoons rum or brandy
1¼ cups wine or sherry
2 cups butter or margarine
2 cups self-raising flour
1¾ cups muscovado sugar
10 large or 12 medium eggs
A few drops almond essence
Finely chopped nuts (optional)

Wash and grind the currants, raisins and prunes and put into a large, clean jar. Add the citron or mixed peel, a little sugar, mixed spices, rum or brandy and the wine or sherry. Leave all these covered for anything from 2 weeks to 3 months — the longer the better. Before mixing the cake, grease and line a 25cm (10″) baking tin with a double layer of greaseproof paper and set aside. Sieve flour. Cream the butter and sugar adding 1 egg (beaten slightly if possible) at a time. Mix these to a creamy consistency and add the fruits from the jar. Slowly add the flour, essence and nuts (if desired). Mix well, adding 15 – 30ml (1 – 2 tablespoons) sherry if the mixture is too stiff. It should just fall off the back of a spoon, but should not be too runny. Put into the prepared tin and cover loosely with foil. Put the mixture in a pre-heated oven at Gas Mark 3 (325°F, 160°C). Bake for approximately 2½ hours until the cake is firm and springy. Leave to cool overnight.

Christmas in the Philippines

Christmas in the Philippines is centred very much around the church. For nine days before Christmas, dawn Mass is held and then culminates with a midnight Mass on the 24th December.

In preparation for this festive season, lanterns are constructed out of bamboo and coloured tissue paper, in the shape of a star, and hung up by a window on the porch. This is then lit up inside with an electric bulb. 'Maguey' trees, well known for their perfect shape, are painted white or green and then decorated into Christmas trees.

Two or three days before Christmas, 'sinuman' and 'patupat' (rice cakes) are prepared and cooked to give as presents to visiting friends and relatives.

The midnight Mass on Christmas Eve is a grand affair with all the pomp accorded to a very special religious event. After the Mass, the 'noche buena' or midnight meal is shared with family and friends and small presents are given to the children.

Christmas Day is the start for carol singing. For the next 12 days the children and organised youth organisations go carol singing around the town and in the villages. Gifts would vary from money to sweet rice cakes, or live chickens or fresh fruit. Any gift received would then be divided among the carolers or served together at an organized party.

On the whole, Christmas is a period of carol singing and parties. This would continue in the New Year where it is celebrated with firework displays and family parties. The whole celebration culminates on the 6th January, when children make their last effort to go carol singing and pester their aunties and uncles to give them more 'pamasko' or presents.

Filipino Christmas star

You will need the following:

10 long sticks (bamboo if possible) of equal size
5 short sticks (equal size)
String or wire
Glue
Coloured tissue paper

1. Take 5 long sticks and arrange them into a five pointed star, each stick overlapping the other, and tie each point firmly with string or wire.

2. With the other 5 long sticks, make a second star. Place it on top of the first and tie each of the 5 points together.

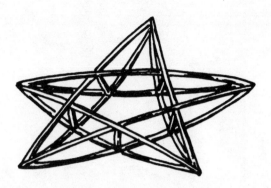

3. Open the star by fixing the 5 short sticks in between the inner meeting points of the star. (See diagram.)

4. When the star is fixed open, cover it carefully with coloured tissue — glue the paper onto the framework. Then the star can be covered with cone or triangular shaped pieces of tissue, with a lotus flower shape in the middle: The lotus shape can be a different colour so it will stand out.

PLAYER A.

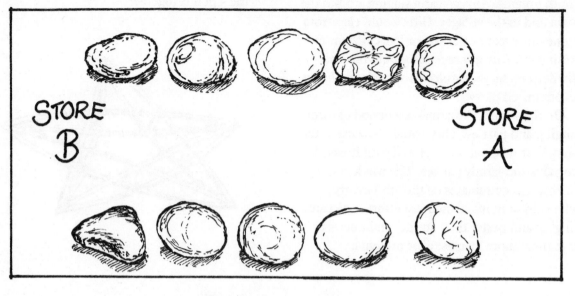

STORE B

STORE A

PLAYER B.

Filipino Sungka game

Aso called *Conglak* or *Dakon*, this is a board game for two players played in Indonesia and the Philipines. The same game, under different names, is played all over Africa and Asia. In Indonesia the game uses a wooden board and cowrie shells for counters. Other places use carved wooden counters or small stones.

You will need:

70 small counters — these can be made from clay or modelling material, or you can use buttons, pebbles or tiny shells.
Clay or modelling material for the board.

To make the board and counters:

First decide what you are going to use for counters. If you are using modelling material, roll out about 70 small balls, leave them to dry and then paint them bright colours.

To make the board, roll out a slab of clay — or make up a block of modelling plaster — approximately 40cm long and 15cm wide. It should be about 5cm thick. At each short end make a hollow large enough to hold about 40 small counters.

Make five more hollows along each long side, taking care that each hollow is directly opposite one on the other side of the board. Leave the board to dry, then paint or decorate it.

To play the game:

2 players sit on opposite sides of the board. Each player uses one of the hollows at the short end of the board as his or her store. The aim is to get as many counters as possible into your own store.

Start the game by filling each hollow on the long sides with five counters. The starting player takes all five counters from any of the hollows on his or her side of the board and, moving round the board clockwise (to the left), drops one counter into each hollow including his or her own store but never placing a counter in the other player's store. Wherever the last counter drops, the player can then pick up all the counters from that hollow, leaving it empty, and then continues round the board as before. If the final counter falls into an empty hole then that player's turn is over but he or she can take all the counters from the hollow opposite that empty hole and place all these counters into his or her own store. A player's turn is also over if he or she drops the last counter into his or her own store.

The game finishes when one of the players has no more counters left on their side of the board and can no longer move. The winner is the player with more counters in their store and on their side of the board.

7. KWANZAA

26th December – 1st January

As a Kenyan who has experienced four Christmas holidays in the West, my experience of these seasons has been, "Oh no, it's Christmas again, I have to send Christmas cards and gifts".

My dilemma, other than money, has been what kind of a gift to get people. To me, in the West people receive gifts from day one of their lives — birthday, valentine, mother's or father's day, anniversary, Christmas and other gifts. So, for me, the kinds of gifts I think of because of my background are either out of place or people already have lots of them. What they don't have is too expensive for them to get themselves, let alone me.

My own family experience until recently had been that I only received gifts as clothes passed down to me. Because we still believe in 'Sunday best', if I got passed-down clothing I would think about what to wear on Christmas Day. Clothing would be passed down sometimes several months before Christmas and, because they were new to me, I would not use them until Christmas day. (This was on condition I did not grow — 'height-wise' or even weight.)

'Kwanzaa' brought home to me memories of family, extended family, neighbours and the whole community spending time and eating together. In Kenya during this season the whole country is generally on holiday except for the essential services and other skeleton staff in offices.

Like 'Kwanzaa', when New Year comes you've eaten all the chicken: a delicacy in my ethnic group and others.

We will have visited with family and friends, and the sick or unwell in hospital are remembered too. Portions of home-made food are taken to them so they can share in celebrations. At home the emphasis is on sharing whatever you can offer, a bit like the 'pot-luck' concept. You bring what you can, and time can flow as we socialize and be together.

As I understand it, 'Kwanzaa' emphasizes this side of cultural values — family, community, and sharing. The name itself comes from my language Swahili and means 'first fruits'. For in Africa this is a time of harvest festivals rather than the cold winter of the north.

As initiated by African-Americans, it is a seven day holiday with seven candles to light and several essential principles. These are known as the *Nguzo Saba* and include:

Unity;
Self-determination;
Co-operative economics;
Purpose;
Creativity;
Faith.

On the final night a feast called the *Karamu* is shared. By then all the candles will be lit in a *Kihara* or candelabrum, and a decorative straw mat will be adorned with fruit and vegetables. The Swahili greeting "Habari gani" is exchanged.

As a cultural rather than a religious holiday, 'Kwanzaa' can include ethnic Africans of different faiths. It relates to the past heritage of African-Americans in a living way, and to the present Kenya I know.

Habari gani!

Zippy Shiyoya.

NEW YEAR

Jehanne Mehta

1. The old year shakes his hoar-y head for his time is near-ly through. We'll see him swift-ly on his way sing a wel-come to the new Now the glass is tur-ning Set the boats a-bur-ning New songs to be learn-ing New roads to be trea-ding.

2. The January wind is come,
   To sweep old lines away.
   The new year comes with pen in hand,
   To write another play.
   Time's at a beginning,
   Set the wheels a-spinning,
   New kites to be flying,
   New links to be tying.

3. Now take your loved ones by the hand,
   For this I tell you true:
   The gladness of the passing year,
   Sheds a glow upon the new.
   Down the road together,
   Sun or bitter weather,
   New feats to be daring,
   New ale to be sharing.

8. CHINESE NEW YEAR

The Chinese New Year

In the days before the new year arrives, trains all across China are packed with people rushing home — the young coming home from distant universities, grown-up sons and daughters setting off to visit parents far away, eager soldiers on long-anticipated leave for an annual family reunion. Young, old and in-between, New Year is the time of year when Chinese everywhere come together, when families are made whole again, new friendships made, and old ones renewed. It is a time, too, for sumptuous feasts and lion dances, stilt-walking and acrobatics, special once-a-year pastries, and dragon dances — a whole year's worth of merry-making rolled into a few festive days.

Guan dong, an otherwise ordinary-looking sweet made of cereal, has, for one, earned an extraordinary place in the history of the holiday. In past times, Chinese families traditionally maintained a small shrine on its brick stove. Inside the shrine was a piece of red paper painted with the image of the kitchen god, who was believed to go to heaven to report the good and bad behaviour of the family to the Jade Emperor, the supreme deity of Taoism, on 23rd December. People traditionally bade him farewell with a pair of lighted candles and a few plates of food and fruit set before the shrine — and indispensable among them was *guan dong*. On New Year's eve, the ritual was observed again to welcome the god back. The ancient ceremony is no longer performed today, but *guan dong* remains a festival favourite, and it continues to go on sale in December as it always has.

Meanwhile, people begin to decorate their homes with *nian hua*, special New Year's pictures of a fat baby and a carp, signifying wealth and abundance, or of the dragon boat regatta. People also tack to their doors red scrolls with couplets that express hope for the year to come. This custom derives from the centuries-old practice of hanging on the door a pair of wooden boards drawn with the portrait on *Men Shen*, the door god, to prevent evil from entering the home. In time, the fearsome deity was transformed into poetry.

On New Year's eve, the family will traditionally gather at table for a lavish dinner. Afterwards, they will often talk or play games until the early hours. In the east China provinces of Jiangsu and Zhejiang, people commonly keep a pair of red candles lit all night while they sit around a charcoal fire, singing or beating drums and gongs until morning.

Outdoors, meanwhile, firecrackers will racket the whole night long.

The origin of firecrackers is lost in the mists of time. But it seems that in ancient times mountain dwellers set bamboo on fire to make it crack, to intimidate the devils whom they believed brought malaria. With the invention of gunpowder, the bamboo was replaced with the powder-filled paper cylinders that we know today.

Chen Wei.

Activities for Chinese New Year

The dragon procession is popular on New Year's eve because the dragon signifies good fortune. Another favourite is the vigorous lion dance to drum beats and music, for the lion may represent valour and strength or energy. In traditional times, branches of sesame, fir and cypress would be burned to mark the passing of the year. Children who go to bed during the nocturnal celebrations may find gift envelopes under their pillows on New Year's day morning. These are red paper envelopes with beautiful gold writing and decoration which contain a traditional money gift as a wish for future prosperity. These red packets may also be given to unmarried relations and to participants in the dragon dance. Red is the colour of good luck and joy. Money is given in even numbers by custom.

The traditional New Year greeting is "Kung hay fat choi" meaning "Wishing you to prosper." The first official three days of the New Year are particularly important for celebration and activity, but the festival really continues until the lantern day almost two weeks later which marks the return of light and spring. You will find this in the beginning 'Spring' section of this book.

A dragon wall frieze may be made using the children's hand prints to look like scales. Make it big and lively!

Banners or scrolls made from red paper can decorate the doorway to the classroom or home. Gold paint or black felt tip pens may be used. If a parent or friend can come in to demonstrate Chinese calligraphy on these, so much the better! Possible sayings to use in a traditional sense could be:

"Success in all endeavors."

"May you have peace and health in four seasons."

"May your happiness be as wide as the sea."

"May all your comings and goings be peaceful."

Make the tissue paper fish or carp which Chen Wei mentions above as decoration.

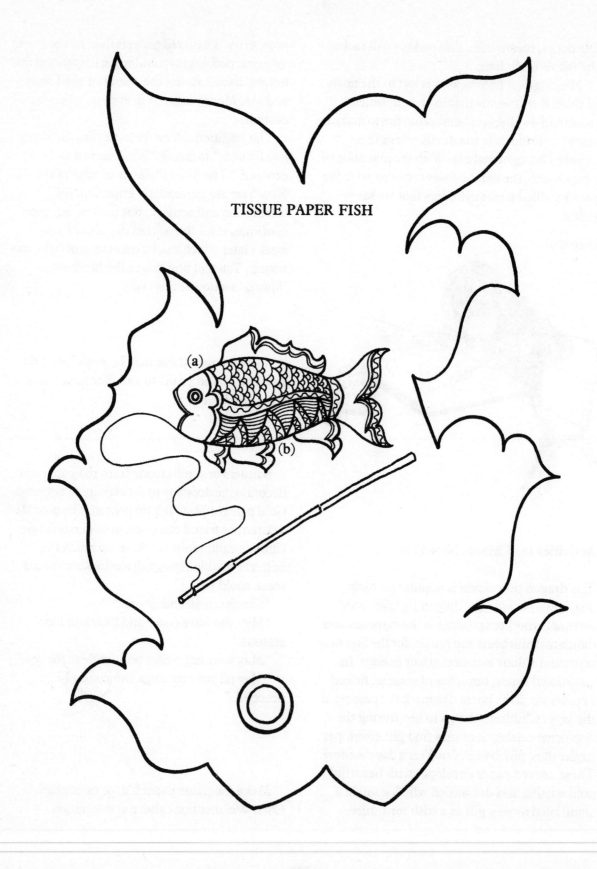

TISSUE PAPER FISH

(a)

(b)

Tissue paper fish

1. Make a card pattern of the fish.
2. Using two layers of tissue, chalk or pastel fin and scale designs on each of the outside layers. Cut out your fish shape after decorating.
3. Glue a narrow strip on edges (a) and (b). Blow gently through to separate the layers of the fish.
4. Glue or staple a narrow strip of paper around the inside of the mouth to hold it open.
5. Using sellotape, stick a cotton thread on the mouth end and fasten to a small cane of bamboo or to a firm twig length.

This will fly well when you run around outside as the fish fattens out and flaps. Make it float and swim through the air!

New Year envelopes

Little red, shiny packages with gold lettering are traditionally filled with sweets or money and tucked under pillows for the children to find on waking.

A sheet of bright/shiny red paper (A5).
Oddments of gold paper or a gold pen.
Strong glue.
Scissors, pencil and ruler.
Sweets or coins to fill the envelope.

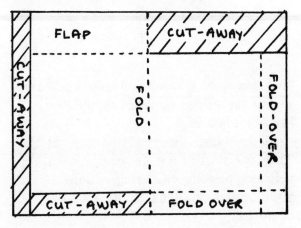

Fold the paper in half, cut off the strips as shown in the diagram.

Fold over the marked edges and glue down firmly. Fold down the flap. Decorate the front with gold pictures or messages. Fill with coins or sweets. Give to someone special.

Happy Chinese New Year

Good Luck
(dai gutt)

The familiar greeting "Kung hei fat choy," means 'Happy New Year,' and recalls the five blessings of luck, food, long life, health and peace.

The Chinese New Year story

The New Year was drawing near and twelve animals were arguing because each animal wanted the year to be named after himself.

You can just imagine the commotion as tiger, dragon, snake, horse, ram, monkey, ox, cockerel, hare, dog, pig and rat argued and argued.

The dragon and the tiger argued over which one of them was the fiercest. "This should be called the year of the dragon because I can breathe fire," roared the dragon.

The horse came galloping in. "No, it should be called the year of the horse, because I can run fastest."

The proud cockerel was preening himself.

"No, you are both wrong, it should be called the year of the cockerel because I am the most handsome animal."

All the animals disagreed with cockerel. There was such a noise of roaring, hissing, neighing, bleating, chattering, barking, grunting and squeaking that the gods were disturbed.

The gods appeared in the sky and demanded to know what all the noise was about. The animals were so surprised to see the gods that they stopped arguing. "What are you arguing about?" asked one of the gods. All the animals

tried to answer at once. The noise was deafening. "Be quiet, at once!" ordered the gods. "You all have very bad manners." The animals were ashamed of themselves. They politely explained one by one what they had been arguing about. Each animal explained why he was the most important and why the New Year should be named after him.

The gods thought hard about the problem and decided to involve all the animals in a race. "Can you see the big river?" asked the gods. "You can all race across the river and the first animal to get to the other side will have the New Year named after him."

All the animals agreed to the race; secretly each one thought he would be the winner. The animals lined up along the bank. "Ready, steady, go!" shouted the gods. There was an enormous splash as all the animals leapt into the water.

The race was very close to start with as horse, dragon, tiger and ox swam neck and neck. However ox was the strongest swimmer and he began to take the lead. Rat was not a very strong swimmer but he was a very clever animal and as soon as he saw ox take the lead he knew he would win the race. "He's not going to beat me," thought rat, "I have a plan." Rat swam as fast as he could and just managed to grab hold of ox's tail. He carefully climbed onto ox's back without ox noticing him. Ox looked around but did not see rat on his back. "I'm going to be the winner," thought ox, "I am well ahead of the other animals, no-one will catch me." Ox slowly and confidently waded the last few metres to the

was tenth, dog was eleventh, and pig was twelfth and last. "You have all done well," said the gods. "We will name a year after each one of you, in the same order that you finished the race."

bank but clever rat leapt over his head and onto the bank first. "I'm the winner, I'm the winner," squeaked rat. The ox was so surprised. "Where did you come from?" he asked rat.

The gods declared clever rat the winner and named the New Year after him. "Next year will be the year of the ox," because ox was second.

One by one the other animals reached the bank. Tiger was third, hare was fourth, dragon was fifth, snake was sixth, horse was seventh, ram was eighth, monkey was ninth, cockerel

All the animals were exhausted but quite happy with this decision so they didn't need to argue any more.

Which Chinese year were you born?

Some people believe that the year in which you were born will tell you what kind of person you are.

Find the Chinese year you were born in by looking at the following list. This will tell you in which Chinese year you were born and something about your personality.

1st. The year of the rat:

| 1948 | 1960 | 1972 |
| 1984 | 1996 | 2008 |

Rats usually sleep all day and hunt at night. A person born in the year of the rat, during the day will have an easy life. A person born this year during the night will have a life full of hard work.

2nd. The year of the ox:

1949   1961   1973
1985   1997   2009

An ox is a strong and faithful animal. A person born in the year of the ox will have a happy, successful life.

3rd. The year of the tiger:

1950   1962   1974
1986   1998   2010

The tiger is an honest animal who takes care of his family. A person born in this year is likely to be intelligent and do well in life.

4th. The year of the hare:

1951   1963   1975
1987   1999   2011

A person born in the year of the hare is likely to have many children and lead a happy and successful life.

5th. The year of the dragon:

1952   1964   1976
1988   2000   2012

The dragon likes to take life easy. A person born in the year of the dragon may like the night time. People born in this year may get very angry when their children are in danger.

6th. The year of the snake:

1953   1965   1977
1989   2001   2013

The snake is thought to be firm, quick and wise. A person born in this year is likely to work very hard and be able to tackle many different jobs.

7th. The year of the horse:

1954   1966   1978
1990   2002   2014

The horse is a friendly animal. A person born in the year of the horse will be strong and enjoy doing good.

8th. The year of the ram:

1955   1967   1979
1991   2003   2015

The ram is thought to be a very proud animal and a good leader. A person born in the year of the ram will enjoy helping others.

9th. The year of the monkey:

1956   1968   1980
1992   2004   2016

The monkey is nimble and usually busy at work. A person born in this year may be curious and find it difficult to mind his own business.

10th. The year of the cockerel:

1957   1969   1981
1993   2005   2017

The cockerel is an early riser. A person born in the year of the cockerel may be proud and industrious.

11th. The year of the dog:

1958   1970   1982
1994   2006   2018

A dog is known as man's best friend. A person born in the year of the dog is likely to be a good friend and quick to learn new things.

12th. The year of the pig:

1959 1971 1983
1995 2007 2019

The pig is an intelligent animal but is inclined to be bad tempered. A person born in this year is likely to be a good parent but may get angry very easily.

Chinese almond cakes

Hsing jen ping:

2½ cups (500g) flour
¾ cup granulated sugar
¼ teaspoon salt
1 teaspoon baking powder
¾ cup soft margarine
1 egg
2 tablespoons water
1 teaspoon almond extract
⅓ cup blanched almonds
1 egg yolk
1 tablespoon water

Sift together the first four ingredients. Mix shortening and egg until creamy. Add water and extract; mix well. Add flour mixture gradually, stirring with fork until dough draws away from side of bowl. Knead to blend. Chill for one hour. Form dough into 1" balls.

Flatten to ¼" thickness. Place on greased cookie sheet, ½" apart. Press almond in each. Brush with egg yolk beaten with one tablespoon water. Bake in 350°F oven for 25 minutes. Makes three dozen.

Honied walnuts

2½ cups (250g) walnut halves or pieces
¾ cup honey
1 tablespoon lemon juice
1 teaspoon soy sauce
Caster sugar

Combine honey, lemon juice, soy sauce and add walnuts to mixture, stirring in well. Let stand two hours, stirring occasionally. Then drain walnuts, and toss in caster sugar. Coat well. Put walnuts in hot oil (shallow fry) and cook until just golden. Drain well.

Delicious with drinks or as an after-meal snack.

Roasted soy bean nuts

T'san tou:

1 cup dried soy beans
3 cups water
4 tablespoons oil
2 tablespoons salt

Wash soy beans; place in a large bowl; cover
with water; soak overnight. Remove from
water; rub with cloth; spread out on a tray.
When skin of beans is dry, place in baking pan.
Sprinkle with oil, coating beans evenly.

Preheat oven to 350°F. Place pan on middle
shelf. Roast until beans turn brown, turning
and shaking beans frequently. Sprinkle with
salt. Serve as a tidbit.

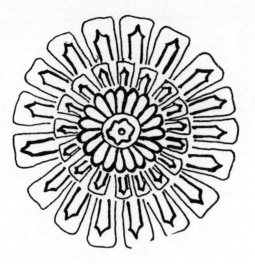

The return of spring

"It is not always easy for a non-Chinese to understand the full moral, social, personal and indeed, cosmic significance of Chinese New Year.

"Morally the keynote is renewal. The old year goes, and with it go old misfortunes and old wrongs, the new year comes and brings the chance of starting afresh. Socially it signifies reunion, the end of strife, the renewal of harmony. Personally and in business one hopes to pay off one's debts, tidy up all loose ends, and turn over a new leaf."

In traditional thinking and in the ancient (universal) experience of the coldness and scarcity of winter, it is a festival strongly connected to the return of spring.

And so we come full circle… from winter's darkness to the renewal of spring and the ongoing cycle of the years' *Festivals Together*.

RECOMMENDED READING

The Buddhist World, by Anne Bancroft, Simon and Schuster Young Books, 1992. Campus 400, Marylands Avenue, Hemel Hempsted, Herts. England, HP2 7EZ.

Christ Legends by Selma Lagerlöf, Floris Books, 1984, 21 Napier Road, Edinburgh, Scotland.

Easy To Make Decorative Kites by Alan and Gill Bridgewater, Dover Publications, Inc. 1985, 31 East 2nd Street, Mineola, New York, 11501, USA.

Exploring Indian Crafts by Manju Gregory, Mantra Publishing Ltd., 1990, 5 Alexandra Grove, London, N12 8NU, England.

Festivals, Family and Food by Diana Carey and Judy Large, Hawthorn Press, 1982, 1 Lansdown Lane, Stroud, GL5 1BJ, England.

Festivals in World Religions, ed. Alan Brown (Shap Working Party) 1986, Longman Group Ltd., 5 Bentinck Street, London, WIM 5RN, England.

The Folk Art of Japanese Country Cooking by Gaku Homma, North Atlantic Books, 1991, 2800 Woolsey Street, Berkeley, California, 94705 USA.

Folk Customs at Traditonal Chinese Festivities, Qi Xing (Translated by Ren Jiazhen), Foreign Languages Press, Beijing 1988, Distributed by China International Book Trading Corp., (Guoji Shudian), P.O. Box 399, Beijing, China.

Judaism in Words and Pictures by Sarah Thorley, Religious and Moral Education Press, Pergamon Press PLC, Headington Hill Hall, Oxford, OX3 0BW, England.

Let's Co-operate by Mildred Masheder, Peace Education Project, 1991, 6 Endsleigh Street, London, WC1H 0DX, England.

Muslim Festivals by M. M. Ahsan, Wayland Ltd., 61 Western Road, Hove, BN3 1JD, England.

Spinning Tales, Weaving Hope, ed. E. Brody, J. Goldspinner, et al. Stories for World Change Network, New Society Publishers, 4527 Springfield Avenue, Philadelphia, PA 19143, USA.

West Indian Folk Tales by Philip Sherlock, Oxford University Press, 1966, Walton Street, Oxford, OX2 6DP, England.

A zen story

The Japanese word zen — ch'an in Chinese, dhyana in Sanskrit — has the meaning 'meditation'. It is the aim of zen, through meditation, to enable a realization of what Buddha experienced in freeing the mind.

Two monks were arguing one day about a flag. The first said "The flag is moving."

The other said: "The wind is moving"

Another monk overheard them as he passed by. He told them "Not the wind, not the flag, but the mind is moving."

Ekai, *Zen Flesh, Zen Bones*, Penguin 1975.

POSTSCRIPT

We hope that you have enjoyed *Festivals Together*, and that you will return to its pages again and again in years to come!

Many of the celebrations in *Festivals Together* are based on festivals occurring within different communities in Britain. Therefore, while we have tried to represent traditions from many different groups, we are aware that there is a huge diversity of cultures whose traditions are not adequately represented in this volume.

Whatever community you belong to, and whatever part of the world you live in, we would be delighted to receive your ideas about celebrations and festivals. We would like to hear your special traditions, recipes, stories and games, so that we may, with your help, create another book of festivals to inform and inspire others — or even just to raise a smile!

Please do send us your thoughts and ideas so that we can, *together*, generate another valuable project.

Write, fax, or even telephone:

Hawthorn Press,
Hawthorn House,
1 Lansdown Lane,
Stroud, Gloucestershire,
United Kingdom. GL5 1BJ

Telephone or fax (0453) 757040.

THE AUTHORS

Minda Anzar Weston is a Filipino who now resides in England. She teaches at Widden Primary School, Gloucester, where she is Co-ordinator for Health Education and Humanities. Many of her pupils use English as a second language, and the school retains lively links with a community in Gujarat, India. She has one daughter, Claudia.

Sue Fitzjohn is Headteacher of a large primary school in the County of Hereford and Worcester. She has a particular interest in religious education and is motivated by the conviction that there is much to be learned from a diversity of faiths. She and her husband, Peter, have one daughter and one son, Sarah and Matthew.

Judy Large was born in the USA but has lived in England since the 1970s, when she studied at the School of African and Asian Studies, University of Sussex. She teaches in adult education and is interested in prejudice reduction and conflict resolution. She and Martin are parents to Abigail, Daniel, Nathan and Bronwyn.

GENERAL INDEX

INDEX OF SONGS

INDEX OF STORIES

OTHER BOOKS FROM HAWTHORN PRESS

[handwritten notes:]

Share Everything

Play fair

Don't Hit people

"Say you're sorry
when you hurt
someone"

When you go out in the
world, watch out
for traffic, hold
hands & stick
together

ORDERS

If you have difficulties ordering from a
bookshop, you can order direct from:
Hawthorn Press, Hawthorn House,
1 Lansdown Lane, Stroud, Gloucestershire,
United Kingdom. GL5 1BJ

Telephone & Fax (0453) 757040.

FESTIVALS, FAMILY AND FOOD
Diana Carey and Judy Large.

This is a resource book for exploring the
festivals — those feast days scattered round the
year which children love to celebrate. It was
written in response to questions from Children
and parents such as "What can we do for
Christmas and Easter?" "What games can we
play?" "What can we make?"

*Packed full of things to do, food to make, songs to
sing and games to play, this is an invaluable
resource book designed to help you and your family
celebrate the various festival days round the year.*
The Observer.

200 × 225mm; 216pp; limp bound;
fully illustrated; ISBN 0 950 706 23 X

THE CHILDREN'S YEAR
Stephanie Cooper, Christine Fynes-Clinton
and Marÿe Rowling.

Crafts and clothes for children and parents to
make.

You needn't be an experienced craftsperson to
create beautiful things. This charmingly
illustrated book encourages children and adults
to try all sorts of different handwork, with
different projects relating to the seasons. Over
100 potential treasures are described,
decorations and even children's clothes.

267 × 216mm; 220pp; sewn limp bound;
illustrated; ISBN 1 869 890 00 0